WHAT 'S YOUR URP?

Don't just make a living; make a life.

Andrew Gibson

Woven Word

WHAT'S YOUR URP?

Copyright © Andrew Gibson 2019

ISBN 978-1-910406-93-9

Published by:
Woven Word
An Imprint of Fisher King Publishing Ltd
The Studio
Arthington Lane
Pool in Wharfedale
LS21 1JZ
England
www.fisherkingpublishing.co.uk

Dedication

This book is dedicated to the memory of three special people, without whom I wouldn't be sharing this and who sadly are not here to see it being shared.

To my parents, Mike and Margaret Gibson, who brought me up in a house where to look out for others was the norm. Both worked in caring professions and brought me up to want to help others. I derive the greatest satisfaction when I help people make a difference, and this was instilled in me by them.

To my dear friend and colleague, Greg Vinnicombe, without whom I would not have discovered Solutions Focused Practice. As a Family Support Social Worker, Greg helped families in the most desperate and challenging situations. He was a kind, giving, caring and loving man, and was taken from this world too soon.

This book is dedicated to their memory and is testament to their legacy. It would not exist without them.

'Every journey begins
with a single step'

Lao-Tze

Foreword

I've worked with tens-of-thousands of Business Owners. And one thing I often hear them say is...

"I didn't think owning a business would be like this".

When I ask what they mean, they talk about how hard they find it. How hard it is to win new business. How hard it is to get their work-life balance right. How hard it is to motivate their team to care as much as they do.

And when people find things hard, what do they do?

Well, they look at what everyone else does – to try to learn (ok, copy) from them.

But, doing this means you only see the things they do that are visible. The money-draining marketing. The time-draining social media stuff. And this just makes things seem harder still!

But here's the good news...

Things can be easier than they seem. You can achieve the Business

You can achieve the Business Owner's goal of Easy Growth...
'Winning lots more work, without doing lots more work'

Andy Bounds

Owner's goal of Easy Growth (or, as I like to call it – 'winning lots more work, without doing lots more work'). And that's where Andrew's book comes in…

He's created a simple guide to achieving Easy Growth - so you can generate, and then win, new opportunities without investing hundreds of pounds or hours.

For example, his concept of finding your Unique Referral Point – the thing which is so impressive about you, that people recommend you to their contacts. Get this right, and it becomes much easier to grow. After all, you're getting more warmed-up intros than ever before!

My advice? Grab a cup of tea, a pen and paper, and read this book as a step-by-step guide. Complete his exercises. Then, more importantly, check your answers with other people (because what you're impressed by is irrelevant – after all, you aren't the one paying for it!)

And one final thing – I love how the book starts by helping you balance your home-life and work-life. Why? Because you only have one life. And you want it to be as exciting as possible. Your business is a fundamental part of you achieving this. And this book will give you simple, quick, free and fun ways to do so.

Andy Bounds

Sales and Communication Expert
Best-selling author and international speaker
www.andyboundsonline.com

Acknowledgements

This book has been many years in development, so there are many I would like to thank.

In addition to my late friend, trainer and mentor Greg Vinnicombe to whom this book is dedicated, there are many people from whom I have learned Solution Focused Practice, the thinking style that is essential to the success of this method. These include John Wheeler, Chris Iveson, Mark McKergow, Alex Steele, John Brooker, Steve Flatt, Anne-Marie Wulf, Jesper Christiansen, Alan Kay, Peter Szabo, Kiersten Dierholf, Liselotte Baeijaert, Anton Stellamans, Shakya Kumara, Petra Muller-Demary, Rayya Ghul, Klaus Schenk, Andreas Fuhrmann, Paut Kromkamp, Biba Rebolj, Suzi Curtis, Jim Bird-Waddington, Naomi Whitehead, Tim Newton, and my dear friend, the late Martin Oswin. I save special thanks for Paul Z Jackson as his developing ideas around stories, themes and reputation have helped me directly with the methods shared here.

My coaching journey started formally with the help of Natalia

Fernandez, Paul Squires, Liz Cox, and my many colleagues on the BizFizz project including Celia Hickson, Wajid Hussain, David Humphreys, Ewan Muirhead, Candy Squire-Watt, Robert Campbell, Thelma Vinnicombe, Julie Holt, Paul Webley, Ian Simpson and many more.

My journey through BNI® was started by my friend Jim Reilly, and then ably developed with help from Rick Armstrong, Keeley Edge, Rich Hayden, Paul Campbell, Sarah Birkenshaw, Niri Patel, Nick Forgham, Charlie Lawson, Tim Cook, Phil Berg, Sam Rathling and of course Dr Ivan Misner, the founder and lead developer of this wonderful system. In addition, I have been helped by many colleagues who are fellow members, especially those in my group, Apex BNI in Leeds. These are too numerous to mention, however for all those who have learned this method in meetings or training courses with me, thank you for your input and feedback, and for sharing your many stories with me.

I am also indebted to my many clients and associates who, perhaps unwittingly, have helped me to test and learn the methods in this book. Many have explicitly helped me with contributions and advice, and particularly with encouragement. Thank you.

With thanks to the dedication of the BNI® team, it has been a great privilege to learn from many masters of their craft at conferences both in the UK and around the world. Particular thanks to Andy Bounds,

Verne Harnish, Ewan Sturman, Ian White, Paul McGee, and Dr Ivan Misner, all of whom have inspired and educated me with their conference speeches. Thank you to Andy for writing the Foreword, and to his wonderful PA Emma Thomas for her help and support.

In developing this book, particular thanks go to my friends and family who have suffered endless conversations with me as the themes developed in my mind. Thanks to David Burnard, Jo Shepheard, Owen Charnley, Anthea Kilminster, Emma Maltby, Soraya Madell, Emma Jaques, Ewan Muirhead, Julia Kalenberg, Bart Tirez, Mike Massen, Brian Snape, Celia McDonald and James Lawther for reading early drafts and providing helpful guidance. Particular thanks to James and Christine Lawther for their hospitality in providing me a space to write the first version of this book in peace, as well as lots of gently supportive conversations. James' feedback on the first version of this book was particularly helpful, and has resulted in this second, more focused offering. Thank you.

And finally to my family. To my late Mum and Dad, I owe everything. I wish they were here to see this book in print. To my sister Jenny and her husband Paul, they are an inspiration in business, running three successful companies that unbeknown to them fit the URP model precisely, and provide me with great evidence that this model works well over a long time. They also have provided such strong support and their advice has always been timely and to the point.

To my own family, my beautiful wife and son, Natalie and Alex, the loves of my life. Thank you for everything, now and for ever.

Contents

Introduction

As an outcome of reading this book, you will love Monday mornings. And Tuesdays, Wednesdays, and every day of the week. My friend and mentor, Rick Armstrong, talks about 'The Seven Day Weekend', and indeed Ricardo Semler, CEO of Semco, published a book under this title in 2004 that takes a case study based approach referencing his own corporate experience. This book is intended to help you develop this for yourself on an individual scale, so here is my take on the concept as explained to me originally by Rick.

Most people enjoy doing the things they love doing with people they love being with at weekends, while 'going to work' during the week is a means of paying for the weekend of enjoyment. Even worse, many people reach the mid-point of their careers following this pattern, and then start planning for their retirement which may be in 10, 15 or even 20 years' time. Why put up with this relentless grind when you could spend every day doing the things you love doing with people you love being with? We choose to like or not like the company we keep and the work we do. Once we choose to change our attitude to the thing we are doing and the company we keep we may find we have, by definition, a 7 day weekend.

This book is not a primer for retirement, nor a means of finding early retirement. This is about making a living doing the things you love with people you love to be with. Read this book, and you will have the tools to deliver your own Seven Day Weekend.

The immediate challenge to this is of course, 'But I do what I do because I need to make a living!'. I can't guarantee that all readers will implement the ideas written here while maintaining their current levels of income. By reading this book, I will help you reassess the things you consider important. You may find that by enjoying a seven day weekend, you spend less on weekend activities and holidays as they are no longer the antidote to the Monday to Friday grind.

The first aim of this book is to help you to find a more enjoyable, satisfying, and consciously enlightened way of making a living. I will help you explore your core values, find ways to make more money while doing the things you are passionate about, and to find the people you want to be doing them with. This works whether you are a private business, a charity, or a 'profit for purpose' community company. This will also help if you are looking for a change in career due to boredom or frustration. I can't promise you will make a fortune if you follow my formula. My best hope is that you will notice differences around your own emotional intelligence, personal satisfaction, increased fulfilment, and measurable improvements in health that will follow from all of these benefits. Does this sound too good to be true? Well, I have applied these principles to my own business, and with my many clients for many years, and this has worked every time.

The idea has broad application, however for individuals, the first premise is simple. Stop talking about what you do. Start talking about how you help.

Our culture defines us through the question, 'So what do you do?'. Even from an early age, caring adults showing an interest in children will ask, 'So what do you want to be when you grow up?'. It is perfectly natural to answer these questions with a job title, however there are two flaws with this approach.

First, the title you give yourself will be one small part of the range of products, services, ideas and concepts that exist within the field to which your label belongs. Second, the title you give yourself will be one small part of you, and all the skills, talents, knowledge and abilities you have are not included in one simple label. On the one hand the label is unclear, and on the other it fails to demonstrate your capacity and capability.

As a result of the limits placed on us by our label, defining ourselves by a title actually reduces the opportunity to find new business. The label can even lead to loss of business due to someone else with your label destroying your reputation. For example, Investment Bankers deliver an important service to the economy, not least of which is the successful management of Pension Funds so many millions of people can enjoy a happy retirement. Yet, since the financial crisis of 2008, anyone with the label 'banker', even those kind branch tellers, suffered from abuse and reputational damage as bank customers did not differentiate between one form of banker and another.

In addition to being labelled by what we do, our society seeks opportunity to apply labels for most aspects of who we are. The application of labels is seldom helpful, and indeed often creates images which are deeply damaging. If you are a Muslim reading this book, or if you are a Migrant, you will already know what I mean. The labelling of people by skin-colour, gender, sexuality, religion, neighbourhood, or residential status has been used to classify entire sections of our global society, often to then make decisions that are "one size fits all", and which seldom deliver as originally intended. This book is specifically designed to help you live a satisfying life by moving beyond the labels, and it will focus on the aspect of our lives we spend most time on – our work, or more specifically, the need to make a living. I will focus principally on the context of self-employment, however the principles also apply to your employment. In my honest opinion, it is easier to apply these principles to create your own work in the modern world of zero-hours contracts and ever reducing employee protections. If the employer holds the balance of power in relation to their employees, this book will help you consider an alternative path where you take back control of your own destiny. If you work through the principles I outline here and can then find an employed role that meets more than your basic needs to earn money, then this book will have been useful. Despite the desires of society to assign a simple label and then to make decisions about categories on this basis, there is no one size fits all solution. This book will help each of us find our own unique solution.

We start by tackling the, 'So what do you do?' question.

My proposal is that we should answer the 'So what do you do?' question with a sentence that begins, 'I help…'. Ask yourself the question now, and see if you can answer with, 'I help…', thinking about who you helped, how you helped them, and most importantly the difference you made for them after you had helped. How many different ways have you helped people recently? I am confident you could list 15, 20, maybe 30 or more stories of specific people you have helped, and the outcomes you delivered for them. A part of the help you delivered will have been due to the thing you do, and for which you will naturally be labelled. However a major part of you as a rounded person will be all your other, unquantifiable skills, and this is powerful when unlocked. This is explored elsewhere with two concepts. The first is social capital, a term that captures the benefits that we have from our social networks.

The second is through a narrative based approach by telling stories of how you have helped people, and who you have helped. Fusing the two concepts leads to the idea that your networks convey your narrative, and so combined will develop and promote you in a helpful way. This happens naturally in so many aspects of our lives that we often don't realise it. In this book, we will harness this approach to help develop ways of making a living that are emotionally fulfilling.

The first section of this book will help you understand and develop your social capital with a view to realising the things you want to do, and the people you want to help as much for your own benefit as for theirs.

We will then look at how you use this process to make a living. If you are self-employed, this process will help you to find word of mouth referrals for the help you provide. If you prefer to be employed, you will have a better understanding of the roles that you will find fulfilling – those that deliver a seven day weekend.

One of the keys to unlock this is to work out the times when you are at your very best, your happiest, your most assured. When we engage people to provide us with products or services, we look for suppliers who are confident, passionate, knowledgeable and happy to help. If we are looking for this in others, it is reasonable that others will engage with us if we display these characteristics ourselves. I always ask my clients to tell me what they are passionate about as when they answer, I see the characteristics I am looking for in a potential supplier or associate.

Note that this is not about helping you earn more money so you can spend more on weekends and vacation, or so you can retire earlier or wealthier. If you have gained in non-financial terms through improved quality of life, you will make different choices and your income may not be an issue. By being passionate in all you do, the money will follow, and there will be many intangible benefits that money just can't buy.

For many years, I worked in large corporations in Food and then in Hospitality. One constant was the concept of the Unique Selling Point, or Unique Selling Proposition – the USP. The USP was originally an Advertising Industry construct, trying to find ways of differentiating one brand from another in the minds of consumers. However, in my many years' experience as a business coach working with the self-employed, there is an expectation that a USP is integral to every business plan. In my opinion, there is no such thing as a USP. If you had a USP, you would have 100% of your market (until or unless you were copied). Even Google has only 92% of the on-line search market at the time of writing! There are very few who can claim to be genuinely unique in what they do. Whether we like it or not, someone else will do something very similar, and in most professions, there are thousands of people doing the very same.

Another popular idea is that we all need to find our own 'niche' in the market. I have found a way of doing this that does not require you to have unique products or services.

In this book I propose an alternative that makes it easier for you to find your niche by using your preferred clients and customers to define it. These are people to help who actually need your help. By being more specific about as many characteristics of these people as possible, the process combines the help you provide with the specific people you most want to help. This leads to an opportunity for you to do the thing you are passionate about to the benefit of others. I call this the Unique Referral Point or URP.

While it is impossible to find one thing you do that is unique, we all work with (or want to work with) a unique set of people. These are people we want to help with our products or services, who have needs that we can meet with our help. You have probably already helped people who fit this profile, so you already have credibility in this marketplace. Educate your network to share this narrative and you have your Unique Referral Point, and this makes it easier for you to start or grow your business, charity or service, or to find a career that delivers greater satisfaction.

If you are thinking that you can help pretty much anyone with pretty much anything, that remains the case whether you find your URP or not. The process outlined in this book will help you to find the work that you want, however it will not stop you from receiving enquiries from people about things you might be able to help with. An interesting paradox is that the more tightly you define your URP, the more enquiries you will receive for other things!

The secret is to be specific in everything you develop. The only way we can distinguish ourselves is through working out the specific people we want to help, and the specific ways in which we help them. If we do this for ourselves and work consistently to develop our URP, it will be easier for us to find the people we can help, easier for us to engage with them, and in time, easier for our network to identify others who need our help. Even better, they will have a method of introducing us that is natural, helpful, and so fits with our social conditioning of making helpful introductions when the opportunity arises.

This sounds really simple, and as a concept it is. Yet as I network and meet new people, I find virtually everyone is keen to talk about what they do, and this on its own will not find you word of mouth referrals. Developing this strategy involves following the processes I outline in this book. So far the Unique Referral Point method has been applied successfully for every entrepreneur I have worked with across all sectors, and I regularly hear from people who have taken these ideas, worked with them, and are noticing amazing benefits.

As it draws from my own experience of working with clients and my developing practice, I have written this book from the perspective of the self-employed or entrepreneur. Entrepreneurs develop networks of clients and suppliers, associates, and people they get to know through their daily activities. This network will initially be external, though as their business grows, they may start to form an internal network of colleagues.

The techniques apply also for those who are employed and who are happy to be employed. Depending on your position, your network will be a mix of internal colleagues and external contacts. For internal colleagues, you will have people in your network in positions that are senior, level, or junior to yours. The principles of developing your social capital and your narrative still apply, and developing a set of Unique Referral Points that reflect the differences you make for your employer will be helpful as you make progress in your career. For example, when I talk about 'clients', an employed person might consider their internal clients – their manager perhaps, or another department with whom they liaise.

I hope you benefit from reading this book, and that you find your next small steps towards your seven-day weekend after you have read it.

Your Passion

Are you in love with what you do? Does the thing you do provide personal satisfaction? Are you happy doing your thing for the sake of it, even if there was no money involved to pay you for doing it? I always ask my clients this question before we start working together.

There are numerous studies stating that more than half of the working population are unhappy with their career, their job, or the thing that they do. Reading the studies, there are an infinite number of reasons given for this, however my preference is not to analyse the reasons for unhappiness. I would like instead to propose an alternative based on what works for the millions of people who are happy every day.

Imagine you went to work, did something you loved doing, for people you loved being with, and at the end of the work, you felt like you had made a difference. Now think about your friends and family. Can you identify one person who fits this description? It is likely that you will notice them smiling, laughing and being relaxed. They will be comfortable in their own skin. Other measures of success that are external such as a nice house or nice car may have come their way, however the chances are that they won't worry too much about material things. If you know someone who fits this description, ask yourself, what are they passionate about?

When we are passionate about what we do, that passion will come through in all our activities, and in a work context, in our dealings with our customers. This book is designed to help you navigate this process, however it starts with a simple question:

What are you passionate about?

Simple question – write down the one or two things you do about which you are passionate, which make you feel truly engaged and alive, and which bring deep satisfaction.

Now look at these, imagine yourself doing them, and think about how you feel at that time. What do you notice about yourself? Are you smiling now? Feeling confident, relaxed, happy? If so, and if these are desirable feelings, what would be different for you if you could feel like this all the time? It is these that are the true passions you have, and don't let the need to make money limit you.

I have helped hundreds of clients to realise that if you do enough of something you are passionate about then the money will follow. It may be that you could make more money doing something else, and if it is your burning desire to make lots of money, perhaps this book isn't for you. If you would like to make a living doing something you love with people you love doing it for, then read on.

In this process, there are no wrong answers, just some simple principles, and the first is:

Do what you love doing, with people you love helping, and the money will follow.

There are numerous examples of people who have followed this principle and achieved financial success. Bill Gates was passionate about computers from his childhood, and spent every hour he could learning how to program. Ingvar Kamprad was passionate about flat-packing furniture and great design. Elon Musk is passionate about developing rapid recharging batteries, liberating electric power from the constraints of the charge-station. Jo Malone was passionate about scents and fragrances, and spent hours blending ingredients and making products from her home, overcoming severe dyslexia to follow her passion. Each of these passionate people became entrepreneurs almost by accident when others noticed their passion and helped harness it into a business. For every figurehead, there is a team of people helping. The passion for the product shines through, and the reason for the work i.e. the difference it will make when complete, is the motivation – not the money that can be made if successful.

Gates, Kamprad, Musk and Malone are very rare in that they turned their passions into multi-billion dollar corporations, however this is not a requirement for everyone. We all know people in our network who are passionate about what they do, and when we think of them, it is with a positive feeling. The same feeling we enjoy when we do the things we are passionate about ourselves.

I had a conversation recently with a hero of mine. He is one of the leading lights in Solution Focused Practice (SFP) and has helped thousands of people to make progress in numerous ways using SFP. He works internationally, is a published author, a brilliant speaker and trainer, and is one of the best coaches I know.

We attended a conference in Frankfurt together, and as it was very busy, he and I only had a quick catch up on the final day as everyone was leaving. I needed a favour from him. I was working with a charity (Specialist Autism Services, Bradford, UK) and I was training them in Solution Focused Practice so they could help their members, all of whom are adults with Autism. In my training, I use one of his training videos, and I thought it would be nice if he recorded an introductory video for me that I could use in the training. He was happy to help and recorded a lovely video.

After doing this great favour for me, he then said something that for me was amazing. He thanked me for the conversation we had at a conference the previous year in Liverpool as it had transformed his outlook, and as a result he was happier, more relaxed, and was making just as much money as he had been before.

I confess, I only remembered the conversation briefly. One of the features of SFP is to recognise what is working well, and so we all pay each other complements. I wanted to complement his training videos and let him know I was grateful to use them in my own training courses. This was a natural thing for me to do. I didn't remember helping him, so I had to ask what it was I had said?

He simply told me that I had said the following:

'Do the things you love doing and the money will follow.'

He told me that when we had our conversation, he had been following projects that were likely to lead to money. He had lost sight of doing the things he loved doing. After our incredibly brief conversation, he went back to doing the things he loved doing, and found the money was coming in just the same as it had when he was looking for it.

I follow this principle myself in all I do, and I explore this with all of my clients. I was taught this when I started my professional coaching career as a BizFizz Coach in Bradford in 2007 and I have found it works *in every case.*

The reason it works is very simple, and there are numerous quotations from through the ages to support it. As far back as Confucius who said, 'Choose a job you love, and you will never have to work a day in your life', through to the 20th century author M Beck who said, 'The way we do anything is the way we do everything'. If you are in love with what you do, and you live it and breathe it when you do it, you have found the perfect place for professional and personal fulfilment.

Now, I can't promise this will work for everyone, however I spend a lot of time working with clients who would like to start a new business. Some of the most interesting conversations have been with the members of Specialist Autism Services in Yorkshire. I always ask them to tell me the thing they love doing, and then I ask them how they feel when they are doing it. With neuro-typical clients (i.e. those who do not have Autism), I might not go into their feelings, however with Autistic clients, this has produced some fascinating responses.

When one described how he felt as he drew his client's on-line gaming avatar, he described a feeling of calmness. When another spoke about racing go-karts, he described feeling positive, presenting himself better, and feeling confident. It was clear from both of these examples that the feelings expressed were desirable and were not how they felt when they were doing something else.

Most people can detect the signs and signals that are shared when we interact with others. If you love doing the thing you do, that will come across. Perhaps you will be calm, or perhaps positive, well presented and confident. If you are, it is likely that the person you are talking to will receive these signals and will be reassured that they are talking with someone who knows their subject.

Ask yourself this question:

What do I love doing?

In Mansfield, a BizFizz colleague of mine, Steve, was approached by a client who wanted to start a new business as a painter and decorator. As a good coach, Steve established that his client's reason for this was that the local council was offering start-up grants for new businesses, and he wanted to access one of these to get started. Something in the conversation told Steve that his client wasn't passionate about painting and decorating, so just to sense check this, he asked what his client did for fun outside of work. The client's face lit up; he was a passionate hang-glider, and not only that, was a qualified instructor. He spent his weekends flying and training others, and it was clear that this was his passion. When given the choice, he would far prefer to make his living doing this, however he didn't think that the local authority would have given him a grant to pursue such an unusual business. Of course, Steve helped his client to progress an application, secure a grant, and start his hang-gliding school where he was able to do what he loved doing with people he loved helping seven days a week.

It goes without saying that there are few hang-gliding instructors in the Mansfield area, yet there are many Painters and Decorators. Steve's client might not have had a large market to go for, however he was assured of a large share of that market by being passionate and highly qualified. Entering the competitive marketplace of painting and decorating while not being passionate would have resulted in the opposite outcome, and a life of simply existing during the week so you come to life on the weekend. Is that the way you want to live?

The People you are Passionate about Helping

Having explored your passion for doing something, with all due respect, I might have just asked you to focus now on developing a great hobby! The next stage is to think about the people that you would like to help. If we can find people that you can help by doing the thing you are passionate about, we have made a small step to starting to earn some income.

Who do I love helping?

I expect that many of you have answered this question with, 'Anyone I suppose'. This makes a lot of sense. If the thing that you do is helpful to everyone and anyone, then in principle, you could love helping anyone.

I sometimes find I ask this question and people tell me of the people that they *don't* want instead. This is useful to know, however it is hard for me to extract the people that you don't want from the universal population of 'anyone' and still find people for you to help. It is easier for me to think of the people I know that you want to help and there are some clear benefits to being more focused.

Ask again, who do you love helping. For example, do you love helping elderly people, or helping children? Do you love helping young parents, or people with no children? What about your desired customers' approach to life? Do they need to share your values for you to want to help them? If so, what are your values, and how will you know when someone else shares them?

There are an infinite number of possible combinations of adjectives, so let me help you.

Thinking of the last time you did the thing you are passionate about, has there been an occasion when you helped someone else with it?

Describe the other person, and list as many of their characteristics as you can. (Keep asking yourself 'What else?' until you have a long list.)

The next question is – would you like to help more people like those you have described now?

This is a simple principle – if you find something that works, do more of it. On this occasion, we have worked out the thing that you are passionate about doing, an occasion when you did it to make a difference for someone else, and then the characteristics of the person or people you helped realise that difference. What are the chances that there are more, similar people who would like a similar difference? We are on our way to finding some customers.

Let's just apply another sense check. When thinking about this occasion, and thinking back to the time you have just recalled, how did you feel? If the feelings were positive, what did you notice about yourself that told you this was a positive experience? List the things you notice about yourself (and keep asking 'What else?')

Looking to the person helped, what did they notice that told them you were passionate about the thing you did for them? What else? List them too, and keep asking, 'What else?'.

Now look at the list of differences you have noticed. Are there any other times when you notice these? What are you doing then? If it is something other than the thing you have identified as your passion, perhaps these are ways of delivering the differences you seek for yourself, and these may be activities that are easier for you to deliver for others.

A Driving Example

A young man I supported in this way was passionate about Racing Cars. His stated ambition was to be a Formula One driver. He absolutely loved racing cars and had raced go-karts in the past. Unfortunately, he told us that he couldn't do this professionally as he didn't have a driving licence. It was also highly improbable that he would be able to get one.

So what do we do here? We have an impossible dream. Well, we followed the process.

Me: 'So how do you feel when you race go-karts?'

Lewis: 'I feel confident.'

Me: 'And what do you notice about yourself when you feel confident?'

At this point, Lewis's body language illustrated the things he said he noticed, as if suddenly receiving an injection of confidence:

Lewis: '*I straighten my back, I project more, and speak more clearly.*'

Me: 'Are there any other times when you notice these things about yourself?'

Lewis: '*Yes – when I am with animals, and when I finished year one of my college qualification.*'

On further exploration, it transpired that Lewis has completed year one of an Animal Husbandry qualification, and he loves working with animals. While it would be impossible for the racing career to deliver the feelings he wants, he worked out for himself that the same differences would be delivered by pursuing his activities with animals.

So, no matter how impossible or impractical your passion is, if you think about the differences you notice about yourself, and that others notice about you, then you can find lots of ways of delivering these. Also, by being aware of these differences, you will notice them happening when you start following your passion into helping others, and you will notice the complements and feedback that you receive that relates to how you want to be.

It all starts by defining what you are passionate about, and then thinking of ways that this makes a difference for others, and ultimately for yourself.

ACTION POINTS

Write down the things you love doing.

How do you feel when you are doing these?

What to you notice about yourself when you feel this way?

What do others notice?

Can you think of an occasion when you did these for someone else, or when someone else benefited from your activity?

How did you feel on that occasion?

Describe other occasions when you notice these differences.

And so on…

The Help Principle

I have met thousands of people who can explain at length their skills, qualifications, how they go about delivering their services, and often, how they are different from the many others who can do similar things. This is very interesting (sometimes!) but it is not very helpful to me. Unless I am prepared to spend a long time in conversation so that I can get a real understanding of what you do, I am never going to be confident that I can introduce you to my network and find you some business opportunity. As a result, the introductory conversations we might have will be something like:

- *'Good to meet you – so what do you do?'*
- *'And good to meet you – I'm an accountant. And what do you do?'*
- *'Great - I'm a business coach. So how's business?'*

And so the conversation will go on. Business will probably be good, or 'very busy', and after a while, the topic of conversation will change to something safer. Even worse for those just starting out, the next question is often:

- *'So how long have you been doing that?'*

For anyone just starting, this is a tough question to answer as how long is long enough? And does the questioner mean how long in total, or how long self-employed? I met a young graphic designer recently, and she was nervous about finding clients as she was only in her twenties, and so felt that clients wouldn't take her seriously. She regularly found herself in the situation outlined above, and sharing the length of her experience was not helping her to find more work.

So how about if we change the conversation just slightly by focusing on the help we provide:

- *'Good to meet you – so what do you do?'*
- *'And good to meet you – I help businesses to manage their finances and pay less tax. And what do you do?*
- *'That sounds interesting. I help businesses grow their sales and profits'*

The logical extension of this conversation is 'So how do you do that?' which then enables an exploration of what each other does, however while one is explaining, the other will be thinking of specific people who might need that help. In this case, there is an opportunity to explore how the accountant can help the business coach's clients to pay less tax as they grow their business which could be of benefit to the coach for one of her clients, and so could lead to an introduction. If you simply state what you do when asked, it is not obvious how this could be helped to happen. By talking about how you help people opportunity flows.

When exploring an opportunity, the thing you do is irrelevant to the initial conversation. What is important is the credibility that comes from demonstrating the ways in which you have helped others to good effect. Referring back to the young graphic designer, in her career, she has helped major high street retailers, and one company in particular she helped with a major re-brand where she designed their new logo. That high street retailer is listed on the FTSE-100 and is well known for delivering growth in challenging markets, partly through their re-branding. When you know someone has this level of credibility, what difference would their length of self-employed experience make?

For example, 'Pink Elephant Consultants' is a company I have made up. Their service is lending their clients elephants that they have carefully painted pink. The elephants are to be placed in reception, and there is a guaranteed uplift in sales of 40% after six weeks. Let's look at the scenarios:

So what do you do – I do this...

- *'Good to meet you – so what do you do?'*

- *'And good to meet you – I install pink elephants in the reception atrium of large companies.'*
- *'Really? So why do you do that?'*

In this made up example, the other party will probably want to know more and will ask questions such as 'Why?'. The answer may come, 'Because we can improve our clients' sales by 40% in six weeks this way', however the prospective client will now take some convincing and will be looking at the idea from a sceptical position.

Now let's role play the second scenario:

So what do you do – I help by...

- *'Good to meet you – so what do you do?'*
- *'And good to meet you – I help companies improve their sales by 40% in a six week period'*
- *'Really – how do you do that?'*
- *'I install pink elephants in the reception atrium of large companies.'*
- *'Fascinating. So how does that work?'*

I have shortened the likely conversation. The key point is that the Pink Elephant's representative has started with how they can help. Having answered, they can then give examples of companies where this technique has worked, and so their credibility grows. The evidence is enough for the other party to be interested, and as we will see later in this book, this opens up the possibility of a useful introduction being made to someone who wants a 40% uplift in sales, and leaves all options open in their mind about how this can be done.

The Opportunity Paradox

Conventional wisdom is that by talking about everything you do and demonstrating your range of expertise through length of service and qualification, you will find more opportunity to do more for more people. The more people you identify who know about and might need your services, the more opportunity you will have to make a difference. If you are specific about 'what you do' then this will limit the opportunity you have to do it for others. However, there is a problem here. The 'doing' approach develops narrow thinking where you think of doing your thing for the same people that others are doing similar things for already, and so you try and find your niche by doing your thing differently. This then leads to attempts to compete on price, service, branding, marketing spend etc, and this is costly and ineffective for most participants in the specific sector. This also leads to a wide scope approach to your marketing activity which is likely to lead to higher costs, and to a broad range of enquiries from across the marketplace that will be hard for you to manage efficiently as you adapt to each specific request.

By focusing specifically on how you help and the specific people you help, the opportunity to help others actually grows. And the paradox is that the more specific you are about who you help and how you help them, the easier it is to find market sectors where no-one else (or at least very few) are competing. And further, the more specific you are, the more you will be noticed, and the more enquiries you will receive from people interested in whether your help will apply elsewhere.

Example - Video Gaming for the Elderly

The video gaming market is a huge component of the entertainment industry, recently overtaking film production in terms of revenue generated. Most games are marketed at an enthusiastic group of young to early middle-aged, predominantly male customers. So how could you expand sales into the grey market, attracting the elderly and infirm to grow your business? With a small group of delegates selected entirely at random, we came up with a solution using the Help process in a workshop format.

I often explore this with teams in a workshop. We usually end up with a business idea, here is one that worked through to an interesting proposition. The discussion is summarised below.

Tell me what you do?

-   We develop video games

How does that help people?

-   Helps with brain training
-   Helps with digital dexterity
-   Helps with relaxation
-   Play for fun
-   Helps with socialising through on-line connection
-   Helps with mental stimulation through creative play

Who needs that help?

-   The elderly
-   People in care homes
-   People in long term residential care
-   People who are isolated

Where do we find these people?

-   Care homes
-   Charities
-   Hospitals

- Clinics
- Social Clubs
- Community Centres
- Churches
- Friends and Family

How should we approach them?

Let's contact Care Home managers and ask them 'Could we meet for a coffee sometime? I have an idea that might help your residents to socialise, keep their brains active, and help them with relaxation. Can I come and pick your brains to see if you think it would work?'

Outcomes

In a very short process, we have established that the elderly and infirm often need social contact, mental and physical training, relaxation, fun and creative play or problem-solving puzzles. We have a product which delivers all of these, so the match is ideal. Working through this process gives us a way of introducing ourselves to our target clients in a way that they should find helpful, and therefore to which they should be receptive. The actual product we are offering is not important in the initial approach to the prospective client. If we could help the elderly and infirm with their list of needs by installing a pink elephant in reception, and if we could present a credible case that this would work, the care home manager will still be interested in talking with us about this fascinating idea.

Now, compare that approach with an initial contact of the traditional approach. Imagine the call…

'Hi, can I come and meet with you to discuss my new video games please? I think they will be great for your residents and I'd really like to come in and pitch my products to you.'

If you were the Care Home manager, who are you going to see for coffee?

How does what you do help people?

As is clear from most conversations about 'work', we can all be experts at defining what we do. Each of us brings a lifetime of qualification and experience to every situation, and we are all comfortable sharing these with anyone who asks. As a result, many conversations focus on what each person does, limiting the opportunity to take these skills and do them for more people.

The first stage of the Help process is to work out exactly what you do and then how that helps others. Let's start with an example that will be familiar to most of us – the plumber.

Most of us will have need of a plumber at some stage, and to help us to choose their services, plumbers are usually very informative about the services they provide. I often see liveried vans, printed leaflets or business cards that look something like this:

ACME PLUMBERS

Specialists in:

- Boilers
- Central heating
- Bathrooms
- Kitchens
- Radiator Flushing
- Radiator Balancing
- Thermostats
- Drains
- Hot Water Storage Tanks
- Taps and Showers

This is an impressive list, and I am sure there are many other skills and services that could be added here. The thing is though, I honestly don't know if I need my radiators flushed, or if they need to be balanced. The good news for the plumber is that their customers have the ability to work out what they need because when you need a plumber, it is usually for one of the following outcomes:

1. A warm house
2. Warm water from the tap
3. No leaks
4. New bathroom/kitchen/WC

When we are looking for a plumber to help us, it is because we need to address one of the short list above i.e.

1. Our house is cold
2. Our hot water is cold
3. Our system is leaking
4. Our bathroom/kitchen/WC needs to be replaced

In many ways, tradespeople are very fortunate when it comes to their marketing. Even though most of their customers won't have a clue what they actually do, plumber's customers have made the connection between the help they need and the service a plumber can provide to deliver that help. As we will see later, trades people are in the minority. It is highly unlikely that the outcomes you deliver are obvious to everyone if you are in the service sector for example. A simple sense-check. Think back to the last time you told someone what you did, and their next question was a guess at what that meant to which your answer was, 'well, not really' or similar polite correction. Is that a regular occurrence? If so, your customers are not capable of working out the help you provide from your title, so we need to find a more useful way of structuring our conversations and activities.

If you are reading this and you are a trades-person, or you think your label helps you get business, the reverse of the above process is also true. The business opportunity you receive from your label alone is likely to be the same, simple stuff. Plumbers receive enquiries to service the house boiler every October (in the UK) as people switch on their central heating and find a problem. How does the plumber change their customers' behaviour so that they are engaged in boiler servicing throughout the year? More importantly for the sanity of the plumber, how do we raise the level of business opportunity to more complex and better paid tasks?

I am lucky enough to know a young plumber I will call P. P was keen to work with more Commercial clients, and he and I had a short conversation about this. I asked him to tell me a story about someone he had helped recently who was in a Commercial business. P told me that he recently helped a printing firm with a full climate control system that combined heating with air conditioning to provide a temperature and humidity-controlled environment. This is a significant step up from plumbing work as I understand it. So I asked P what difference this made to his client. P told me that the greatest levels of waste and inefficiency in printing come when the ink to paper process is affected by the local atmospheric conditions. By accurately managing the print room climate, P was able to improve the printer's efficiencies and reduce their waste levels. If P shares that story through his networking and other marketing, he will soon find referrals to printers looking to save time, save money and make money – and the revenue generated for P's business will increase as he works on more complex and higher value projects.

The Customer Service Paradox

We are quite likely to speak with friends, neighbours and family to seek a recommendation. And what are the criteria we use to make a recommendation when asked? They are nearly all service related for example:

ACME PLUMBERS

Specialists in:

- Turning up on time
- Working quickly
- Not making a mess
- Leaving the site clean and tidy
- Being knowledgeable and giving good advice
- Doing the job well

Not one of these service related items has anything to do with the technical skills, qualifications and experience of the plumber. Those are taken for granted as basic levels of competence if you are to be referred from one client to another. What matters is that you can help, and you can help with a high level of customer service. The Customer Service Paradox is quite simply that it is rare for a client to have a complex technical understanding of what you do, and to then make a qualified recommendation on that basis. If your friend seeking a plumber asked you about their specific skills, you would rightly state that you didn't know. You will only notice the observable elements of their work, and these are listed above. Again, this makes it hard in most sectors to be recommended on the basis of what we do and is the reason why so many companies invest time and money in promoting their excellent customer service offer as a point of distinction from their rivals.

To apply the Help process to a plumber therefore, the liveried van and marketing materials should say something like this:

ACME PLUMBERS

Specialists in:

- Keeping you warm
- Keeping you clean
- Keeping you dry

These are the basic needs that a plumber will meet for their clients on a daily basis. More importantly, if you are good at these three things, your clients will be very happy to recommend you for the one that you fixed for them.

Here is an example conversation that is perfectly natural and will lead to more business for the plumber who keeps you warm:

- *'Brrr – it's a bit chilly in here'*
- *'Yes it is. The heating's on the blink and I need to get someone to look at it'*
- *'Good news – I have the contact details for a plumber who specialises in keeping you warm'*
- *'Great – could you please introduce me?'*

Becoming known for how you help people leads to more referrals. Once you have been put in touch with the client, your skills and expertise will be with you in the room, and to find out which of these you need to deploy, some structured research will be required.

Now let's look back at our friend P. His help statement could be:

- 'Helping Printers Save time and money by reducing waste and improving efficiencies'

Notice that there is no mention of P being a plumber here. The label, 'plumber' is like the Pink Elephant in my imaginary consultancy firm. Leading with the label will put people off making contact. Leading with the benefits, the help provided, will encourage people to find out more, and if the first thing they hear is the story of help provided to another, then the label becomes less of an obstruction to a useful conversation.

Explore the needs of the client when you meet them

Working out how you help people is the first stage, and I have deliberately used an example that applies to the domestic situation of most people who will read this book. It may not be obvious about how you help people, however using the plumber as an illustration should help you to start this process for yourself.

The second stage is perhaps a very simple one for the plumber, though again it may not be immediately obvious. There are simple situations leading to simple solutions, and then of course there may be more complex needs leading to more involved projects. The only way to find out is to explore the needs of the client fully when you are conducting your research.

Our friendly plumber will be very familiar with this stage. In the vast majority of cases, a simple 'so what seems to be the problem?' will elicit the information needed for the plumber to focus their attentions on meeting the need in hand. This is where 'the house is cold' enables the plumber to check the boiler, the radiators, the pipework, the thermostat etc. It would be a rare occasion when a client specified to the plumber that their house was cold 'and they therefore needed the radiators to be flushed and balanced'. That is the skill of the plumber to diagnose, and then recommend a course of action.

If you don't know, just ask

This stage merits more exploration however, even with a case that is simple on the surface such as the Cold House/Plumber interface. A few extra questions at the start of the process could help to recommend a choice of courses of action which will lead to various levels of benefits, depending on the actual needs of the client.

An experienced plumber will enhance their credibility and deliver a better solution by asking a full set of diagnostic questions. Through this diagnostic process, the plumber can work out a choice of courses of action and then can discuss these with the client before embarking on the one that will meet the greatest number of needs. This is more effective for both supplier and client, and following this process means that the client will choose the best path they can *afford*, not simply the cheapest course of action.

So how do we broaden this out to a process that works for all organisations? The answer lies in developing a set of diagnostic questions for your own circumstances that focus on the solutions and outcomes that the client is looking for.

In the dim and distant past, sales people were tasked with selling and the most enthusiastic took this to heart. Venturing onto a motor dealer forecourt was a terrifying process as there was a likelihood that you would be approached by a salesman (usually a man) who would try and steer you in the direction of a specific car that they wanted to sell because it would meet their needs, not because it would meet the needs of the customer. A lot of cars were sold by this method, however the process was stressful, and 'second-hand car dealers' were tarred with a reputation. Thankfully, sales methods have moved on, and the approach is now completely different.

Whenever a help based conversation takes place, the priority task is exploration of the needs of the client. In vehicle sales, the best motor dealers have trained their teams so that the process has been revolutionised. The sales people will now make a point of introducing themselves to the prospective customer, and then leaving them alone to browse in peace. If the customer chooses to engage a sales person, the conversation will be about the needs and priorities of the client and then vehicles will be suggested that will be a match for the customer's needs. If a sale is concluded, the customer is likely to be happy with their purchase, and there is a likelihood that they will tell their friends how happy they are and recommend the vehicle dealer as a result.

If you understand how you help people, your conversation with a prospective client should be along similar lines. Most of the initial questions at this stage are intended to gain information so, generally, they will begin with 'What'. Here are some example questions that may apply to different situations, and which will lead to insight and information that will help you to work out the needs of the client:

- *'What you are looking to achieve overall?'*
- *'What objectives have you set (or been set) for this project?'*
- *'What are the overall corporate (or department) objectives?'*
- *'What other resources or activities will contribute to this?'*

In addition to this, there are questions to establish quantities and expectations, and most of these will be started with 'How':

- *'How does this project fit in with overall corporate (or department) objectives?'*
- *'How will you/we monitor and evaluate this project?'*

Once initial information has been gathered, and expectations have been explored, there are some more excellent questions that you can ask that will flesh out more context and more detail, and this is where you will start to get really valuable information:

- *'How will you know when the project has been successful? What differences will you notice?'*
- *'If we were sitting down in 12 months and reviewing a successful project, what differences would we be celebrating?'*

Listen for detail and you will find the opportunity

The more detail you can extract about the needs that are there to be met, the better able you will be to deliver the solution that will meet or exceed the needs of your client.

It therefore makes sense to develop as clear an understanding as possible about how the client would like things to be after your intervention. One of the most powerful questions you can ask to develop this is quite simply, *'What else?'*.

Often, the first answer to a question is not the most helpful, nor the definitive response that you need if you are to develop solutions together. Asking 'what else?' or similar, and often asking this many times, will produce a longer list of information which will be very useful when developing or delivering a project.

For example, if you go to the Doctor, you are looking for specific help with your specific problem. It is up to the Doctor to ask enough questions to make a diagnosis, and then to prescribe the best course of action. Similarly, in business, it is essential that you gather enough information so that you can establish as many of the known needs as possible at the start of your project. This will help you to deliver a far more effective solution for your client which will be to all parties' benefit in the long run.

There is also a bonus to your credibility if you spend time exploring the needs in full. First, the greater number of needs uncovered, the greater the chance that you will not only be able to meet some of them, but will also have demonstrable experience of meeting something similar for another client. Second, by identifying a list of needs, you will be able to prioritise using the likely impact and urgency to determine which you should tackle first. You may also identify some quick wins that you can implement promptly and easily. This is only possible if you explore all of the needs and listen carefully to the client when making the first steps towards a possible project.

What do your clients want?

As an example, many years ago, I helped a local charity who had asked me to give them some advice about fundraising. They help children to improve their reading skills by offering direct one-to-one support, and they produce training workshops to help teachers as well. While they had a lot of success and a great track record, they were struggling to make progress in growing their client base as they were seen as a cost by the schools they were targeting. Their approach had been to try to speak with head teachers at local schools. As anyone knows who has tried this, head teachers are very busy and are constantly targeted by sales people. As a result, they have a very effective set of filters to prevent any sales call from ever getting past their receptionist team, so this approach was hard work and unproductive. We needed to find another way.

The conversation I had with their Chief Executive took about 45 minutes and here are the edited highlights:

- *Coach – 'Can you describe your services to me?'*
- *Client – 'We help children to improve their reading skills through direct support, training workshops for teachers, and production of materials to support home activity'*
- *Coach – 'So who benefits from this?'*
- *Client – 'Children benefit through improved reading skills and increased reading age'*
- *Coach – 'What differences do you notice when this happens?'*
- *Client – 'Children are less disruptive in class and perform better in exams'*
- *Coach – 'Apart from the child concerned, who else benefits from this?'*
- *Client – 'Well, if there is less disruption in class, then everyone can study properly, and the overall standard of exam grades will increase.'*

- *Coach – 'Ok, so if the overall standard of exam grades increases, who benefits'*
- *Client – 'The children themselves, and of course the school – it will get a better OFSTED report and will attract more pupils.'*
- *Coach – 'Is there a financial benefit to attracting more pupils?'*
- *Client – 'Yes – the pupil premium that comes with each pupil will allow them to access a bigger budget, and if their OFSTED is improved, more people will want to send their children there.'*
- *Coach – 'So who benefits from increased budgets and better OFSTED reports?'*
- *Client – 'The school staff, the head teacher in particular.'*
- *Coach – 'Who else benefits if there is less disruption in class and the children perform better'*
- *Client – 'The parents of the children will be pleased as their children will have better exam grades'*
- *Coach – 'And where can you access parents at a school?'*
- *Client – 'On the board of governors, at the school gates, through community activities, events, virtually anywhere'*
- *Coach – 'So how could you approach a school now?'*
- *Client – 'I could try and find out who was on the board of governors, and talk to them about better exam grades for their children and a better OFSTED report and bigger budget for their school'*
- *Coach – 'And do you think they would be interested to hear from you?'*
- *Client – 'Absolutely!'*

In this short conversation, we worked through to see who benefited. We managed to find a financial benefit which is very important if you are asking someone to pay for your services. If you can make a case based on saving money or making money, you can legitimately ask for a share of that to pay for your services.

Whatever service you are providing, you can go through this process. Here are some short examples:

Professional Service	*How you help*
Accountant	'I help people to pay less tax'
Business Coach	'I help people to make more money'
Marketing Consultant	'I help people to make more money'
Data Protection Consultant	'I help people to comply with the law and to avoid large fines, saving them time and money'
IT Consultant	'I help people to improve productivity and customer service, reducing costs and making money'
Personal Assistant	'I help people spend less time on admin, helping them to do more of the things that make them money'
Travel Agent	'I help people save time and money on business travel, helping them to be more productive'

When you read these statements as a client, the natural question is to ask 'How do you do that?' and this is the opportunity for you to tell a story about how you have helped someone similar, and the outcomes they enjoyed as a result as a great way to explain your services in a bit more detail. This is not the opportunity to provide a long list of services in the hope that the client needs some of them!

There are some services where the opportunity to help people is fairly obvious. If an Accountant tells you that they can save you money on your tax bill, that is pretty clear to most people.

Who do you really help?

For example, I recently met with an HR Consultant. They described themselves as having a portfolio career as they were doing other things as well as HR Consultancy in order to make a living. In our first phone call, simply by asking about what was in the Portfolio and then asking 'what else?' a few times, I found out that they are a specialist in the area of maternity and are highly qualified to advise companies about how to manage maternity issues both before, during and after. This is a significant step up from my own understanding of HR consultants. Suddenly, I can think of loads of clients where they have had maternity issues who would love to hear from them. Also, there will be HR Consultants who *don't* have that expertise and may be interested in calling them in to train and advise them, or in support of specific clients. By specialising, it is easy to find referrals, and to become known as the expert in your specialism.

Of course, the same rules apply to my maternity consultant colleague as to any other service provider. Ask yourself the following questions to work through this process:

1. How do I help people?
2. Who would benefit from that help?
3. Who else?
4. Can we keep finding benefits for others until there is a financial benefit?

Repeating this loop until you find ways in which you can help specific people save money, make money, or save time (often enabling them to make money) is the key to finding clients and developing a strategy to approach them.

Applying to Products

The process applies to products, however the work that goes into working out how you can help people should translate into your marketing activities as well as direct sales. Whatever you are trying to sell, it is incredibly hard to distinguish your product from your competitors'. In a product business, it is still possible (though very rare) that you will come up with a product that is both unique and marketable. However, most businesses offer products that are similar to their rivals', and many try to distinguish by product attributes such as reliability, quality, ethical values, or simple cost. If you refer back to ACME Plumbers, this is taken for granted now, and so 'our great customer service' is no longer unique.

In the days when these attributes were uncommon, this strategy would work well, however in the 21st century, every product is expected to have these attributes, so how do you develop your specific offer to be different from your competitors?

If you follow the help process outlined in this chapter, it is easy to define the ways in which your products help people and then you can feed this into your marketing plan. For your product, it should be possible to identify:

1. The needs that the product meets
2. The people who have those needs
3. Where to find those people, and especially those who can afford your product.

This should help you to be more targeted, and if the materials and copy you produce are based on the help your product provides, you are more likely to engage with your target market in a way that is lower cost, and higher conversion for a given spend.

Action Points

Work out how the thing you do helps, and who it helps.

If you have already helped people, who did you help and what with?

Practice telling the good stories you have about how you have helped people.

If you have a small number of examples, where can you find more people who are similar and who might have similar needs?

The Power of Being Specific

Before we start thinking of our business-selves as suppliers to our clients or customers, let's picture ourselves in their shoes. We receive goods and services every day, and there are many occasions when we are very specific in our needs.

- When we go to bed at night, we set an alarm for a precise time to wake the next morning;
- We maybe start the day with a hot drink. Whichever we make, we know how we like it. If we are ordering in a café, we will ask for it just so;
- We look at our diaries to find our first commitment of the day. Normally, we will note down the time, the location, the others involved or the task to be done. We will normally allocate a duration too.

So as consumers, we are good at being specific. Yet when I ask business people and entrepreneurs what they do, and who they do it for, after they have told me their trade or profession, the answers are nearly always, 'Anything for Anyone'. If we applied this approach to the three every day examples above, what happens:

- Before I go to bed at night, I will set the alarm for anytime.
- As you walk into your favourite café, you address the Barista with, 'Hi, can I have a drink please?'
- 'I know I have a meeting today...'

The above examples are deliberately silly just to make a point, however the second one is a genuine business conversation. If you walk into your favourite café and ask for 'a double espresso with a shot of hot milk', you will get exactly that. If you need a quick hit of caffeine and this is your preferred option, you get the outcome you want. And in coffee culture, the outcome of a quick hit of caffeine is so popular, every culture has a name for this exact drink. Variously, you will find this described as:

- A Café Cortado (Spain - coffee cut with milk)
- A Café Pingado (Portugal – coffee with a drop)
- Un Café Noisette (France – tricky, however noisette usually means 'small and round', perhaps referring to the shape of the drop of milk)

And my favourite

- A Caffe Macchiato (Italy) where the description can mean spotted or 'stained'.

I love that the Italians would consider adding a spot of milk to an Espresso as 'staining' the pure coffee!

Cafés throughout the world have developed shorthand for their drinks to make it easy for customers to order precisely what they want. As well as improving the outcome for the customer, this also makes it simpler and quicker to serve the drinks, improving efficiencies throughout the company which of course helps profitability. If you can present a simple set of products or services that is manageable within your current capacity, capability and resources, you are a long way to finding some clients who will want what you offer.

Let's look at another example that is much closer to home for most of us.

If you are currently single (or can remember the time before you were in your current relationship) friends will often try and set you up with a possible partner. Imagine the conversation in the shortest possible form:

- *'Hey Andy, I hear you are looking for a new partner. Maybe I can help. Who would you like me to introduce you to?'*
- *'Thanks. To be honest, I'd be happy to date anyone thanks!'*

Can you picture my friend's face here? I can, and I am not sure they are going to be able to set me up with a friend anytime soon… or worse, they are going to set me up with another friend who gave them a similar response!

If you were thinking that this would be OK, you are probably right. Maybe the two people that my friend knows who would be happy dating anyone will indeed be compatible and the match will be a success. To improve the chances of success, would it be helpful for my friend to at least know a little about the partner I was looking for?

Here are some things which might be helpful:

- Gender

If you were genuinely interested in 'Anyone', gender would not be important. For most single people, this is likely to be a significant, deal breaking factor. Here are some other characteristics that may be helpful:

- Height
- Appearance
- Interests
- Education
- Location

It is certainly true to say that the more you can describe the type of person you would like to meet, the more likely it is for them to find someone close to your ideal, and the less time you will spend on dates with people who don't fit the bill. As match.com says in their profile writing tips for new registrants, the more questions you can answer when submitting your profile, the more likely they will find you a match. The example they use is, 'If you are a lover of Bikram Yoga, can't stand smokers and definitely want children in the future, it is easy to identify potential deal breakers simply by reading someone else's on-line dating profile.' Looking at these examples, it is possible that your views would change over time, and this applies when we are developing our business ideas too. Nevertheless, we have a set of specific customer needs we can help with, so let's save ourselves a lot of time and money by identifying these first, and then approaching that small group of people after.

Let's look at a very specific area that is common to most of us. I hope to goodness this never happens to you, however let's imagine you had a heart problem. To whom would you turn? Well, obviously you would look for the most eminent Heart Surgeon you could find. You would expect them to have spent years performing heart surgery, to be up-to-date with the latest clinical developments in cardiology, and to have reached their eminent position through successfully helping many patients to recover from their heart condition. Would you be happy to be operated on by the doctor who picked up the hospital chart and said, 'Ooh, triple heart bypass! Haven't done one of these for a while, but I'll give it a go!'.

From a referral perspective, if a friend asked you to recommend one of the above surgeons, who would you choose? Exactly, and it is the same in all occupations and businesses. If you are specialised in what you do, the easier it will be to refer to you. Indeed, if you are unique in your chosen field, you will have the pick of every referral and many will come to you first just in case you can help them.

So we have three simple points already just by being specific:

1. What is my specific set of products or services that I want to deliver, and that are within my capability and capacity?
2. What is the profile of the customer or client who needs these?
3. If I can help these customers with my specific products, I will become known as the go-to person for this and I will start to receive more referrals as my reputation grows.

In some lines of work, it will be obvious that the thing that you do is linked to the needs of your clients (or customers, or patients), and so you won't have to do much other than build a good reputation and you will receive referrals for that activity. This works for many professions, and for lots of popular areas. Most people know that they need a plumber to fix their leaking tap, or to service their boiler. However, what if you are a Consultant? Very few people wake up in the morning and have a flash of inspiration that they suddenly need the help of a Consultant! And what if you are a plumber who wants to do more than fix taps and service boilers? If you are operating in a crowded sector, the next way to make yourself more specific is to work out how you help people.

If we take the consultant as an example, consultants often help in very specific ways. When a business owner needs more sales for instance, or when there is a need to make changes to adapt to a changing marketplace, it can be helpful to employ a consultant. If you are marketing yourself as a 'Sales Growth Expert', or a 'Changing Marketplace Adaptation Consultant', you are making yourself more specific in the way you describe yourself, and it is possible that someone will wake up one morning and think, 'I need sales growth – let's google 'Sales Growth Consultants' and see what happens!' This still relies on the customer working out that you exist, and there is a further step you can take. Ask yourself this question:

What are the outcomes I deliver for my clients?

If you look at the consultants above, perhaps they could answer with the following:

- I help business people grow their sales
  or

- I help business people to change their businesses to adapt to market forces

Just making this extra step has probably got you thinking to yourself, 'Who do I know who needs more sales?', or 'Who is facing big change in their market right now?'. By ensuring that you are associating yourself with these outcomes, it is easier for your contacts to find you introductions to people who might need your help. This starts to distinguish you from some of your competition, so we are on the way to being specific.

In the world of business, marketing managers have attempted to identify their products from competitor brands by identifying specific outcomes and then associating their brand through advertising spend. Procter & Gamble, the manufacturers of Daz Washing Powder, have long promoted their brand as the one that 'Washes Whiter', and over the years, their taglines have consistently promoted this message to distinguish their offer from other large box laundry detergents.

From the early 'Blue Daz boils WHITEST of all!' in the 1950s through to the 2000's and the band 'White Said Fred' promoting 'I'm too sexy for my Whites', Daz marketeers have associated their brand with delivering clean, white clothes. This focus on a specific outcome helped them to be one of the top brands for over 50 years in a crowded and competitive marketplace.

Delivering this brand consistently over the years required focus on the specific benefits, and the original team at Procter & Gamble, having found a winning formula when launched in 1953, invested in and developed the formula so that their brand became a household name and their doorstep challenge transcended advertising to become part of the national culture. When looking for your next step, it is always a good idea to look for what is working already and do more of it. If focusing on one key outcome (washing whites whiter) kept Daz in supermarkets for over 50 years, then we can adopt the same practice for our business and expect a successful outcome for ourselves.

There are other benefits of this approach. A moment ago I mentioned that a homeowner with a leaky tap might seek the services of a plumber. This is probably the most basic job in the plumber's lexicon, and as it is normally a simple task, it is unlikely to be a high fee-earner. If you are the consultant heart surgeon of plumbing, specialising in complex heating systems, do you really want to spend your time earning small fees repairing leaky taps? A clear benefit of marketing yourself as, 'helping you keep your house warm' is that you are likely to become associated with that outcome. This helps increase the likelihood that someone with a cold house will contact you. Even better, the more of your network who also associate you with keeping houses warm, the more likely they are to introduce you to someone they meet in their cold property. As well as being more likely to receive enquiries for the level of work you want, you will of course also continue to receive enquiries for leaky taps. If you have associated yourself with a specific outcome, you have earned permission to help directly if you have time, or to politely refer on to someone who is looking to fix leaky taps, leaving you to concentrate on keeping houses warm.

You can go further of course. Describe the houses you help to keep warm. Describe their location. The more characteristics you can identify about the property and the people living there, the more specific you will become. As you build credibility at keeping houses warm, you will start to work in bigger houses and on more complex systems. People will start to refer you to others with large houses and complex systems as they will have stories to tell about how you helped someone in their situation before. Eventually, you will be unable to take the leaky tap jobs, and you will need to refer these on, or take on extra resource to deliver these. Ultimately, if you become the person who specialises in keeping warm retired empty-nesters in rural parts of the country living in thatched-roof cottages with oil-fired boilers how easy will it be for your network to refer you to everyone they know in this situation whenever they visit their house?

If you are looking to work with commercial clients, apply the similar thought process. Like P who we met earlier, marketing yourself as 'Helping Printers Save Time and Money' will generate enquiries from printers who want to save time and money. It really doesn't matter whether your services are plumbing or pink elephant related, you will be given a chance to share a story or two that gives you credibility as having delivered these outcomes for someone else. And it is easier to find these opportunities than you think. Just ask yourself, 'who have I helped recently?' and think about the differences they noticed after you had helped them. Would you like to help more people like them? And if you are not sure what differences you made, however you are sure you helped them, simply get back in touch and ask them. You might be pleasantly surprised, and you will have more credibility enhancing information to add to your story.

The more specific you can be, and the more specific the problem you solve, the easier it is for your network to find referrals for you AND the more likely it is that they are the referrals you want. That sounds like Utopia to me – and if I told you that was where I made my living, by practicing the techniques I am sharing in this book, then welcome to the departure point on the best journey of your life!

ACTION POINTS

What is my specific set of products or services that I want to deliver, and that are within my capability and capacity?

What is the profile of the customer or client who needs these?

What Differences do I make for my clients and customers?

Your Unique Referral Point

So far we have looked at the power of being Specific, the importance of identifying how you Help people, and the vitality that comes from being Passionate about what you do and who you do it for. To really focus on the opportunity that is there for you, we need to combine these three characteristics and look for as much detail as we can. The final element in this process, the one that will lead to you finding and receiving referrals, is to identify the Occasions when your product or services will be needed. Adding the time-related element that means you are contacted when the customer or client actually needs you.

This process is about focusing your activities on finding the opportunities you want. This does not reduce the enquiries you will receive for other things – if anything these will increase as your name is more known for your specialism. The great benefit of being specific and focused on the outcomes you deliver is that when you receive an enquiry you can take the work if you want to or pass it onto a referral partner who is better placed to deliver instead. The advantage of identifying the specific occasions when your specific services or products may be needed is that it further focuses your mind on the opportunities you are looking for, and in turn helps your network to think of you when they find themselves in one of the occasions you have spoken about and with which you are associated. I have decided to call this the Unique Referral Point (URP) – the antidote to the Unique Selling Point which doesn't exist for virtually all businesses, no matter how many business advisers and business plans ask for it!

Being ultra-specific about all aspects of your services will help your network refer to you with confidence, and you can rest assured that they will ask you when they are not sure. Remember the consultant heart surgeon? They will receive referrals for cardiac surgery all day long. Yet they will also receive enquiries from friends or colleagues about other medical matters for two reasons: first, they are respected experts in their field so they may know about other, simpler matters; second, they are respected experts in their field, so the chances are they know other respected experts in other fields and therefore can pass a high quality referral to the right person. It is more efficient and effective for you to have the choice to help or to pass to another better placed than you. If you are in the 'anything for anyone' market, it is so much harder to say to someone 'no I don't do that' without drying them up as a source of referrals in future.

In the 70's and 80's, a leading drinks brand chose to market under the slogan 'Anytime, Anyplace, Anywhere', an approach that was so memorably captured in an advertising jingle for the alcoholic aperitif,

Martini. This brand message accompanied an advert featuring wealthy people relaxing on vacation, usually involving sun, ski or swimming. Relaxing on vacation is a very specific occasion when an alcoholic aperitif may be appropriate and so the logic of their advertisements was impeccable. Sadly, the message made no sense.

Unless you are selling Oxygen or Water, you really aren't available anytime, anyplace, or anywhere. With your own business in mind, it requires large investment to build a brand that is marketed to anyone, and even the largest corporations in the world do not attempt this impossible task. They spend vast sums analysing their marketplaces, their target customers, the reasons for engagement, and the benefits and outcomes for which their customers will actually spend their money.

Despite the popularity of the concept and its frequent appearance in business plans, I firmly believe that there is no such thing as a Unique Selling Point (USP). Even if there was, it is of no value in finding you new business. Virtually no one and virtually no business is genuinely Unique in what they do. To be genuinely Unique, you would have 100% of your marketplace and there would be zero competition for your products or services. One of the most successful modern companies is Google, and even they are not Unique. They have (only) 92% of the on-line search traffic – the other 8% are spread across Bing, Yahoo, plus Russian and Chinese alternatives. So if even Google with many billions of dollars of available cash to invest in their brand can't manage 100% of their marketplace, what chance do we have? As a small by the way, and having been presented with the USP section of many a client's business plan, anything that starts 'we will offer the best customer service' is not unique, and nor is 'we will be the cheapest in the market'.

The second part of this is that the 'Sales' or 'Selling' part of the USP has no value. Ask yourself honestly if you like being sold to. Virtually no-one likes being sold to, so why would you spend time and money trying to find the one thing about your offer that enables you to sell to your target customers? This approach is of limited value, and in my experience, unless you are genuinely unique, you will not receive more referrals due to having a well-defined USP.

We have looked at the importance of being specific, the value of considering your products or services in the ways that they help potential customers, and we have completed a sense-check to make sure that you genuinely love what you do or sell. The final element we need to develop our own Unique Referral Point is the Occasion.

Whenever someone takes action, it is because they had a reason to do this *at the point in time that they did it*. For example, in a modern car there is very little to go wrong, yet we all know we should check the tyre pressures and put screen wash in the reservoir. Our cars are often very helpful with this, providing us with a warning when the levels are low. Yet the time we actually take action is when we spot that the tyre is nearly flat and is bulging at the sides, or when we go to wash the windscreen and no screen-wash comes out. We have been given plenty of notice of the need to act, and it would have probably been more convenient to take action before crisis point, however many of us will wait for the final stage before we take action.

So if your service is pumping tyres, or filling screen-wash, what is the occasion you can associate yourself with? The flat tyre is visible to all. If you become known as 'the flat tyre guy', then not only will people with a flat tyre seek you out, anyone who knows you and rates you will recommend you when they see someone with a flat tyre. We will explore this process in more detail later in the book when we look at the referral process.

For now, the important step in our process of developing our Unique Referral Point is to look at the circumstances and timing, the Occasion when someone needs our product or services.

Here are some examples.

There are some things in life which responsible people just do. These include such interesting tasks as investing in a pension or making a will. Most people know that they should be doing these things, and as many professional will writers will tell you, 'You are never too young to make a will'. Yet the subject of death is something few people want to discuss, and wills are associated with death, so people often postpone the discussions until very late in life. Indeed, the numbers are staggering. According to research carried out by Opinium Research on behalf of Unbiased.co.uk, some 31 million people in the UK were at risk of dying without a will in late 2017. If you are a will writer, surely this is a massive marketplace – just tell them you exist and the people will come running! If this was actually happening, then there wouldn't be 31 million people in the UK without a will, so what can will writers do differently to start meeting this massive need?

Everyone knows they should have a will, and the service offered by will writers is pretty specific. The marketing is often on the basis of how they help their clients – by looking after their loved ones after they have gone. It is fair to say that if you are a will writer, you will need to be passionate about the help you provide and the service you offer as unfortunately the job title is one of those that can end conversations at parties! So what are the Occasions when someone is motivated to take the steps necessary to make a will?

First, let's look at the occasions when it would be helpful to consider writing a will. The greatest need arises when we go through life-changing events. For example:

- Having a child
- Getting Married

- Buying a house (especially with someone else, married to them or not)
- The death of a close family member
- Being diagnosed with a serious or terminal illness

The last one is likely to make a will a high priority, yet the other four should all do this as well. In order to be able to offer their specific help at a time when their clients need it, or even better to be recommended by someone else to the client at their time of need, will writers need to associate themselves with these occasions.

There are many ways in which you can do this, however if you are a will writer, perhaps you have already worked something out that identifying these Occasions has made obvious.

Let's look at the list again.

- Having a child
- Getting Married
- Buying a house (especially with someone else, married to them or not)
- The death of a close family member
- Being diagnosed with a serious or terminal illness

Instead of thinking about the process of writing a will (the 'doing'), let's instead think about the differences that will be realised after the will has been written.

- Most parents will want to pass their estate to their children when they are gone, with minimal disruption and minimal tax liability.
- Most loving couples, married or not, will want their surviving partner to inherit their estate and to live securely when they are gone.
- When living with someone, security of accommodation for your surviving partner is of paramount importance.
- When a close family member dies, the benefits of having a will are clear, and the impact of not having a will even clearer. This is an occasion when it is natural to address your own affairs.
- On diagnosis of a serious or terminal illness, the need for a will is obvious.

The key outcome offered by having a will for the first three of these occasions is peace of mind. It is desirable to know that your estate will be passed to your family or your partner, or to those you deem appropriate. It is also desirable for many to know that the amount taken by the tax authorities will be minimised too. These are very positive outcomes that most people would want, and yet when you ask someone about wills, they will often make a comment about not wanting to talk about dying. Of course, if you wait until you are dying or dead, it might be too late.

I have selected will writers for this process because the normal conversation about the 'doing' is a barrier to new business, and the beneficial outcomes are not obvious to most people (31 million in the UK). This imbalance is the same for all products and services. If you can think of the occasions when your specific services would be most helpful, you are increasing the chances of the introduction being timely and the prospective client wanting to do something with you. No matter what you do, it is unlikely that your prospective customers will want to think about it unless you provide them with really good reasons to do so.

As a step towards your own Unique Referral Point, identifying Occasions is a massive saver of your time and will substantially increase your conversion rate from introduction through to a transaction.

Service providers can take a look at the tactics employed by product marketeers who have been associating products with Occasions for decades. There are the obvious such as the massive boost in TV advertising for perfume in the run up to Valentine's Day, Mothers' Day, and most of all, Christmas. However there are also many examples of marketeers trying to associate their products with Occasions that are not a natural fit. For instance, Kellogg are the largest manufacturer of cereals in the world, however their principle products are known as 'breakfast cereals'. Kellogg have spent many millions trying to associate their main products with other occasions such as post-school snacks, pre-bed suppers, or even as a meal to be taken at lunch or in the evening.

Most entrepreneurs are not global brands, so we need to look at this process for our specific needs so we can plan to spend as much as possible doing the things we love doing to help people we love helping.

When starting a new business, we might be prepared to do anything for anyone, however we are more likely to get our first clients if we think of the occasions where we can help and then try to find people at that particular point in their lives. Not only will this help us find clients more quickly, we will be focusing on the combination of service, help and occasion that makes *us* happy, so we will enjoy the journey from the very start.

When we are growing, we can build our businesses by replicating the successful occasions where we have been helpful. When we have made a successful and repeatable difference on one or two of these occasions, we can make confident steps into new occasions where we can offer the same basic service or product to people under different circumstances. We have a lot of evidence that our specific service helps and so the stretch to a new occasion will not be too great for ourselves, nor for our clients should they have the opportunity to recommend us.

This combination of Specific Help Provided, Specific People Helped, and Specific Occasion when the Help is Needed is combined in what I call the Unique Referral Point, or URP.

Despite the best entreaties of business planners throughout the world, it is not possible to define a Unique Selling Point through looking at your activities in isolation. If, through reading this book, you can define and develop your URP, you can easily distinguish yourself from your competition and will find making a living so much easier. So here is the process for you to work through.

1. Based on my Passion for the thing I do, what is my specific market sector?
2. Based on my Passion to help, who are the people I have helped or want to help?
3. Based on my capacity and capability, what characteristics define my clients?

We are going to work through these together.

Looking back to the thing you are Passionate about, here is my challenge to you. Forget about promoting everything else you do.

It is tempting to consider ourselves to be capable in every aspect of your trade or profession. Remember the plumber's van and the list of services offered? I regularly receive business cards from professional services people where there is a long list of services they offer crammed into the tiny space afforded by their card. Simply applying the 80/20 rule, I know that most of these will be occasional services, and the lower they are on the list, the less likely they are to be the thing you really love doing. So my first recommendation is to stop promoting these, and stop talking about them. Now, that is not to say that you should stop doing those things if you find a client who needs them and you are happy to provide the service. Remember, you will still receive enquiries for those as your URP reputation grows. My proposal is simply that whenever you are asked, 'So what do you do?' you give the 'I help…' answer that fits the thing you are most passionate about doing.

Even within an emerging sector, it is possible to be specific. One crowded and competitive marketplace is on-line marketing, and many people have developed consultancies in this area. While the principles are similar across all platforms, you can use this process to become an expert in just the one platform that will work best for your specific client base. Not only is this expertise valued by your client, it makes it more obvious to them as to the reasons you might be able to help them.

The second aspect of this is to look at the client you have, and the client you want to work for. This is the art of being specific in stating who you help when you are answering the 'So what do you do?' question.

Let's face it, the theory and the practice are two different things, most of us are Martini – Anytime, Anyplace, Anywhere – when it comes to our clients. If we are offering a service or product to consumers, most of us can help anyone, and as long as our service is the one they need, we can help them with pretty much anything too. Throw in the amazing technology that connects us now, and we can often help anywhere as well.

Let's look at another example. If you are a Conveyancing Solicitor, you will receive enquiries from people moving house. You may also receive enquiries from time to time for other property transactions, and these will come simply from the label that is attached to your service.

However, it is hard to make a living if all your referrals lead to a single property transaction. You need a lot of referrals to make money and sustain you and those nearest you. While you develop your reputation through helping lots of clients, you will spend lots of time (and possibly money) on getting the word out that you are a Conveyancing Solicitor looking for business. The opportunities you receive will be more people looking to move house, the most basic service you offer, and for most of your clients, a once only transaction. Let's look at a more specific set of clients who could refer you regularly and apply the Help Process to see if this works.

Most Conveyancing Solicitors would love to receive regular referrals from Estate Agents, so as an example, let's look at how a Conveyancing Solicitor can use the URP process to distinguish themselves from their competition, all of whom wish to work with local Estate Agents.

I worked through this example with a young Conveyancing Solicitor who we will call M. When I asked M how they helped Estate Agents, they told me that they offered a very rapid service that could speed up the process. If all other parties followed the process towards sale without changing their minds, he could help the Estate Agent to speed up transactions.

So what is the outcome that is delivered to the Estate Agent if M saves them time? Well, the benefit will almost certainly be financial. Faster deals mean more houses sold more quickly, meaning more commission income and improved cash-flow for the Estate Agent. This is also good news for the Estate Agent's clients, which will of course improve the whole experience for all involved, reducing failure in the conveyancing system, and improving the reputation of the Estate Agent which will result in them receiving more referrals. In this situation, all parties will be better off, and so M's service is about much more than conveyancing.

Most Estate Agents receive calls from Conveyancing Solicitors asking for referrals. Only M is contacting them offering to improve their revenues and cash-flow.

The third aspect to consider is a range of defining characteristics, and while the list below is by no means exhaustive, here are some to consider.

- What is the size of your ideal client? You can characterise them by headcount, turnover, or perhaps observable characteristics such as the areas they live in or trade from;
- Where are they located? While technology may enable you to work with anyone, anywhere, where do you actually want to work? If you would prefer to work within five miles of your house, that is fine, and this characteristic will help you (and your network) look out for the opportunity you actually want to fulfil.
- What is your preferred method of delivery? If your service is hands-on then clearly you will have specific geographies in mind where you can go to deliver your service. If you are bringing a product to your clients, are you providing that on-line as a download, or via the post? Will they come to you in order to buy, whether on-line or in person? Can you provide your conversations via telephone, video call, or is face-to-face in person the best for you?

The more of these characteristics you can define, the more specific will be your Unique Referral Point. And it is absolutely possible to be 'Unique' through following this approach and to have a number of URP's depending on the situation and who you are talking with.

The URP Pyramid

In most marketplaces, there is a pyramid of service providers which looks something like this:

When we start out, we are one of many Novices. It is quite likely that when asked about the customers we would like, we will happily state we can help anyone with anything they need, such is our enthusiasm just to find paid work. If we are lucky enough to survive in our practice, as we gain knowledge and experience, we make the transition to Practitioner. We notice this when other Novices and some Practitioners start coming to us for advice. We share our stories with them and help them develop their practice. For many, a long career as a Practitioner leads to Expert status where your Experience and Expertise combine, and most Experts make a good living. Progressing through these first three stages usually involves an element of the URP process as clients will recommend Experts to similar clients, so this will happen quite naturally over time.

Some people choose to take this Expertise to a wider audience by delivering training, writing articles and blog posts, or maybe writing a book, all means of finding other ways of offering their Expertise beyond direct contact. At this stage, you have reached the Influencer level where you are not only sharing your Expertise, you are Influencing the development of your practice through your own original thinking and sharing of your learning. Influencers share their Influence by means that enable them to go beyond their personal capacity.

We live in a world where to be an 'Influencer' is the dream of many young people, setting out to ape the financial success of contemporary Instagram Influencers who are paid to micro-blog through this platform. To avoid confusion, the Influencer in my system is one who Influences others in their marketplace through their knowledge or experience, and who shares this with Experts, Practitioners and Novices using means that enable them to go beyond their personal reach. If the Instagram Influencer has built a following based on sharing expertise, they fit this model and most will have a well-defined set of Unique Referral Points that will help distinguish their personal brand from their rivals, and for which their followers will engage.

Then, sitting at the top of the pyramid, there is the Guru. This is the person that the Influencers go to for help, and that all in the Marketplace will look to as the reference point for the practice.

In most marketplaces, there is room for only one Guru, although if the marketplace is large, there may be a small handful, each with particular specialisms or methods to share. Reaching Guru-status means everyone wants a share in your wisdom. They will buy your books, subscribe to your videos, and pay handsomely to spend time with you whether through inviting you to speak at their conference, or through sharing half an hour of your time to benefit from your wisdom. People will follow you on social media, engage with your blog, and share your articles with their own networks.

So who gets all the best referrals? If we can be the Guru in our marketplace, our entire network (and beyond) will want to refer to us. The Guru gets the referrals they want and can take their pick of these, passing on the rest to the Influencers and Experts they are happy to recommend.

Yet, if your marketplace is vast, and there is only one Guru, how do we rise up the pyramid? Do we need to compete in some way to knock the Guru off their perch?

Well, there are two ways of looking at this. You can work hard to be the Guru of your whole profession. With good fortune, hard work, and a lot of time, full market Guru-status will be achieved by maybe five or six people at most during the peak years of your career. As an alternative, more productive, more focused way forward, you can identify the Unique Referral Points you wish to work within, and then become the Guru of a smaller, more focused URP defined Marketplace.

For example, if we look at the will writer's situation, there are 31 million potential clients in the UK right now. Yet we identified that two ideal opportunities for the will writer are when people get married, and when people buy a house. Here are two very specific URP's and when you think about it, it is easy to identify the other professions that are involved in the processes of getting married and of buying a house. If we are known as the will writer who wants to bring peace of mind to people getting married or buying a house, we will get referrals to people on the occasions when the outcomes we deliver arise in a natural conversation. In order to increase the number of referrals we receive from people on these occasions, we need to look at how we help the other services and trades that are involved in these transitional stages.

Applying our URP process at its primary level, we are looking to talk to the happy couple, or the recipients of the keys at very specific times in their lives. To grow the chances of regularly receiving referrals to people we don't know, we need to work out how we help the professionals.

Looking at the process of getting married, there are numerous professionals involved in the process from jewellers, milliners and florists, through to chauffeurs, hotels and churches, so where do we start? Well, if two people are coming together in marriage, their financial situation changes dramatically. The chances are that they will need help from an Independent Financial Advisor (IFA). A will writer can help an IFA to set up trusts and tax efficient vehicles to ensure that the couple's wealth is looked after when they are gone, so there is an obvious synergy with IFAs. For people purchasing a house, the same is true of the many professions and trades involved. Yet in the middle of all of it sits the Mortgage Broker and just like the IFA for the couple getting married, there is a clear opportunity for the Will Writer to help the Mortgage Broker to ensure that the assets against which the mortgage is secured are protected and looked after for the benefit of the family.

Now the thing is that these are fairly obvious links, so let's look for the more obscure. When I look at the list of people involved in the marriage process, the jeweller is an obvious candidate for a discussion.

When the happy couple purchase their rings, they are investing in purchasing assets that they have no intention of selling, and indeed will imagine their children inheriting when they have gone. It is easy for the jeweller to refer to the Will Writer at the point where the assets are purchased. The reason? For peace of mind.

So for the Will Writer to receive referrals from the Jeweller, what must they do? Clearly, they must find referrals for the Jeweller. The more referrals they can give to the Jeweller, the more they will be in the Jeweller's radar when they sell rings to a newly engaged couple.

And by the way, these referrals do not need to arise solely from their will writing activity. Actively seeking the referrals that the Jeweller wants by learning their stories and by getting to know them and their Unique Referral Points will improve the quality of referral passed, and the frequency with which they are found. More referrals passed in both ways will lead to more opportunity.

Apply the process to the people you want to talk to and keep going until you find those where there is a clear benefit of working together. Before you know it, the pyramid is smaller.

If you are developing your connections in the marketplace defined by your URP, it is easy to spot opportunities to rise up the pyramid. You can become an Expert fairly quickly as you develop the methods of engaging with your target clients and develop stories of helping them which you share. You can offer to train people in these methods, or share them on social media or at industry conferences, moving yourself to Influencer within your URP. If you wish to write a book or produce training videos, it is easier to do this on a very specific subject aimed at a very specific marketplace. If your books or videos are taken up by many, or your followers grow beyond all others in your URP sector, you will be on your way to Guru-status. Now, you may not be the Guru of all will writers, however if you are the Guru of will writing for all Jewellers, you will receive referrals from Jewellers all day long, while your colleagues are still looking for the 31 million in the UK by conventional means.

As you might expect, I have used this method myself for many years now, and so here are some of the URP answers I give when asked, 'So what do you do?'

- I help charities and community companies develop sustainable revenues so they are more secure;
- I help charities and community companies deliver sustainable change in their clients;
- I help charities and community companies improve their client outreach and engagement;
- I help stimulate local economies by helping people support others into self-employment in a safe and sustainable way;
- I help people to network with each other effectively;
- I help people who want to start a business to do so within their existing resources so they do it safely and with minimal risk;
- I help CEO's of large organisations to reduce the queries that land on their desks by helping their staff learn how to make great decisions when the processes don't help them.

And so on and so on! My approach on meeting someone in a business context is always to engage with the person I am talking to first and to find out more about them and the people they help. When they ask me about what I do, I can tailor my answer to be relevant to people they might know in their network. As well as stimulating a useful conversation, there is a possibility that they will know someone who might need my help. If I have credibility in providing help to others, they will have all the information needed to make a qualified introduction.

As a final example, a friend of mine, David, has been successfully working this way for many years. Having left multinational FMCG in his late 30's, David decided to apply the Marketing skills he had learned in his own right as a freelance consultant. Many years before I had even thought of writing this book, David worked on the market sector where he had credibility. As a farmer's son living in Devon, he knew he could help agricultural vets to grow their businesses and he has built his business doing this very well across his region. His business was even renamed recently from his original brand, Agathea, to the very specific and to the point Vets Marketing Help. Apart from the evidence of the results he delivers for his clients, David recently found out that others identified him by his URP when he met one of the Influencers in his sector at a conference. After he had introduced himself, the Influencer immediately said, 'Ah, you're the guy who helps vets with their marketing.' Remember, David had never met this man before, yet he knew about him and the difference he made to his clients. This is the next part of our process – using our URPs to help with the creation and management of a referral generating reputation.

Action Points

Identify the following:

The thing I LOVE doing

The people I LOVE helping

The specific characteristics that apply

The specific occasions when people might need you to make a difference

Practice answering the question, 'So what do you do?' with an answer that has the following format:

'I Help <People Like…> with <Specific Product or Service…> that delivers <Outcomes…>'

See how many of these you can come up with that are true to your Passion.

Stories, Themes and Reputation

I love a good story. And as I am human, I am not alone. We are a story telling species and have been since the dawn of time. Indeed, anthropologists estimate that we developed language skills some 700,000 years ago, yet the earliest form of writing yet discovered is called Cuneiform. This has been identified by experts as a means of recording transactions from Sumerian scribes dated around 3200 BC, a mere 5000 years ago. We naturally tell, learn and share stories verbally, illustrated by the story telling nature of simpler societies or 'folk culture' as noted by anthropologists. With the dawn of the interconnected social media age, the quantity of stories is growing exponentially, and across all forms of communication, stories are being told all the time. So how do we manage the stories that are told about us so that they increase the chances of us finding more opportunity to do business? If you follow the process in this book and become known for your passion, the way you help specific people, the outcomes you deliver for others who are your chosen Unique Referral Point pyramid, this task becomes a lot easier.

Let's think about the stories we have heard recently about our friends.

Inevitably, some will be stories of bad news, yet we universally seek to provide a happy ending if we can. To this end, the bad news story about our friend will end with where they sought and received help to resolve their situation. If you are thinking of good news stories, they will be enhanced by inclusion of the reasons they are good news, and often this will be about the difference your friend made in the life of another. Perhaps they provided the happy ending to someone else's bad news? The better the help provided, the more the story will be told. And the more often the context arises, the more appropriate the story, and the more often it will be told in context.

There are many resources available that expand on the art and substance of stories and storytelling, so I am going to explore one specific aspect in this chapter. My friend Paul Z Jackson talks about stories becoming themes through repetition, and ultimately becoming a reputation. So how do you manage the stories that are told about you so that they enhance your reputation and bring business opportunity?

The first thing to be aware of is that to build a reputation, your stories need to be consistent. This involves finding your core values and being true to them in all that you do. If you are true to your values, consistent in your approach, keen to help whenever you can, passionate about the help you provide and the thing that you do, and you always treat clients, suppliers, colleagues and all who interact with you with respect, the chances are that the stories told about you will be reputation enhancing.

Take any one of these elements and demonstrate inconsistency, and your reputation will suffer.

For example, we all have female friends who have felt that a price quoted for some work was higher than the price quoted to their male neighbour. Is that trades person going to be recommended? Or is the story going to be one of 'found out' and the reputation is diminished.

In the social media age, reputations are made or ruined in minutes. Of course, there are terabytes of posts, articles and news stories about the pros and cons of social media. All I will add to this developing medium is that, as responsible human beings, we are in control of the stories we post, or the situations in which we place ourselves where others could post on our behalf. We are also in control of the stories we post about others on-line. We need to be mindful that what we say about others has a direct impact on our own reputation. Before we can ensure that our on-line stories are in line with the reputation we wish to create, we need to work out how to create our own reputation and then the activity to support this process.

Let's start with establishing your core values.

There is an infinite set of core values and each one of us is different. Have you ever thought of yours? It is likely that you will identify with statements such as 'to make a difference', 'to make lots of money', or 'to support my family'. Spend a few moments thinking about what is important to you.

To help turn these into something realisable, let's imagine (or recognise) that you are already delivering your core values. Think of an occasion recently when you felt proud of being true to yourself. Now ask yourself the following, 'What does my partner notice about me when I act in a way that is true to <my core values>'. This can be life partner, business partner, or both. Think of the things they say, or gestures they make. Keep asking yourself 'what else?' until you have a list of the many things they would notice. Ask yourself, 'what else?' a few times, and explore the different values that are important to you.

What about your clients or customers? What will they notice that will tell them you are being true to your core values? If you prize yourself on your customer service, what is it that your customers will notice that tells them this is the case every time?

There are some great examples I have heard, and some of these have been repeated many times at events and training courses I have attended. Some may even be apocryphal, however here goes with one that illustrates my point.

The story goes that a wheelchair-bound passenger was flying Virgin Atlantic to a conference in the Caribbean. Not only was this an important trip where she was speaking at the conference, her wheelchair was specially adapted and it was vital that it was safely transported. After a successful but tiring trip, imagine her horror when she returned to Heathrow, and as she disembarked the plane on the airport wheelchair, saw her own being removed from the cargo hold as a mangled wreck. After years of devotion to another airline, this had been her first experience of Virgin Atlantic. At this point in time, she was distraught, and they were to blame.

The attentive ground-crew took her to the representatives of Virgin Atlantic who offered profuse apologies and helped them get home. On arrival, they noticed a flashing light on their answering machine. The message was from Sir Richard Branson. He offered his apologies, gave them his personal mobile number, and asked them to call as soon as was convenient. As you might expect, she made the call straight-away that evening.

Sir Richard advised her he had been told immediately about the situation, and he wished to offer his own apology. He had arranged for a full set of catalogues to be sent to her house. He asked her to choose any wheelchair she wanted and specify the modifications that would fit her needs. He would ensure that the new chair was delivered to her as rapidly as possible. In the meantime, the Virgin Atlantic team were at her disposal and were to meet her every need.

Following this episode, the customer's next course of action was to change the travel preferences of her organisation so that wherever possible, Virgin Atlantic would be their chosen airline. And with this story now shared widely, how many other people have chosen Virgin Atlantic with confidence when booking their flights?

In this example, it is easy to give credit to Sir Richard Branson, and indeed this story fits his personal brand perfectly. However for me, the real credit goes to the ground crew staff who contacted him, and felt empowered to do so without fear of repercussions. The encouragement to report the issue is to be applauded, and the speed with which they obtained Sir Richard Branson suggests that the corporate culture of exceptional customer service held true throughout.

A long time before I heard this story, I flew with Virgin Atlantic to Johannesburg, South Africa. My neighbour was a lovely woman, a little older than me, on the way to see her children and grandchildren, and we passed the time in conversation. Unfortunately, after dinner, my neighbour felt unwell, and suddenly vomited. She had no time to find the sick bag, and so was now in need of immediate help. With minimal fuss, the aircrew attended to her every need. She was provided with materials to help her get clean, and new clothes to replace those that she was wearing. Her dirty clothes were bagged, and taken away to be stored elsewhere on the plane with the reassurance she would receive them after we had landed. Her situation was handled impeccably, and the Aircrew were empowered to help her with all her immediate needs.

While these two stories are about very specific help provided by attentive ground and air crew, the reputational enhancement for Virgin Atlantic is far greater, and I am confident that in reading these, you will have formed opinions on their hiring policies, training procedures, and whether or not they are a good company to work for, let alone with which to fly.

My friend Bart Tirez works for Familiehulp in Belgium. I saw him deliver a workshop in Timisoara, Romania where he shared the experience of introducing the thinking of Walter Hart and his book, 'Twisted Organisations' (currently not available in English), and combined this with training in Solution Focused Practice from IlFaro in Leuwen, run by my friends Liselotte Baeijaert and Anton Stellamans. Whenever a new recruit joins Familiehulp, they are presented with a thick book of rules, policies and procedures which they are expected to read and understand so they have the answer in every situation. Sound familiar?

Bart is in the process of helping his team to learn Solution Focused Practice so they can deliver the desired outcomes for the client, and not be constrained by the need to follow the system. By equipping his team with decision making skills, he has helped his team of 40 domiciliary care workers to move from a Low Trust, Low Compliance (due to the large number of rules) model to a High Trust, High Compliance (with a small number of rules) model. This has improved their service to their customers and allowed Bart to spend more time on matters of strategy and direction rather than on directly answering queries from his team where they don't know 'the answer'. The whole essence of his work is to be focused on the intention, not the system. Bart's team are focused on the care their clients need, not on the system developed over time by the organisation and delivered in a massive rule book. Without knowing how they did it, it is clear that the same principles apply at Virgin Atlantic on the basis of the two stories I have shared here.

Now ask yourself the question, 'am I being true to my core values?'. Think about the work you do (or want to do), the subject you are studying, the company you keep. If you are happy that you are in a good place in relation to your core values, you are very lucky indeed.

So what are the stories that you want to be told about you, and how do you spread them through your network? If you are thinking of a great set of stories about how fantastic you are, and that the opportunity is there to promote them through social media etc, I am afraid you are going to need to think again. Telling our own story about how great we are is not helpful, and indeed could be dismissed by others as self-promotion. It is far more effective if others are telling your stories for you, and this is where being true to your values is essential.

If you have worked out your Unique Referral Points and made sure that the parameters fit your core values, the more help you deliver for the people you want to help, the more likely it is that stories will start to percolate through your network. Having identified your URP and your core values, you probably have already started thinking of stories that you could share. Remember back to the networking conversation and the 'I help...' format of answering the question about what you do? This is an opportunity to share a short form story related to your URP and core values. If you don't have any credible stories, perhaps because you are now in the process of seeking to help a new set of people that better fits your URP and core values, it may be that you need to test yourself with some people who fit this profile. This is one of the reasons for being prepared to start offering your services simply to gain experience of helping people. It may be that you need to offer your services to people you already know where they are happy to help you develop, and happy to share the differences they notice so you can use this information (perhaps anonymously) to generate credible stories. Another way of looking at this stage is to seek opportunities to 'pilot' your ideas. It is perfectly reasonable to ask for some payment for a pilot if appropriate, and of course if the desired outcomes are not noticed, never mind – it was only a pilot!

As you gain experience, so people will start being helped, and you will be able to share more stories about the people you have helped and the differences made as a result. And if they appreciate that help and find others who need similar help, they will start telling stories to their networks and making introductions for you, supporting the referral with the story of how you helped them, or the person they know, or the story that they heard about you from their network.

This is a slow process, and the length of time it will take will vary. In my case it was around 2013 that I started helping charities and community companies with sustainable revenues and delivering sustainable change in their communities. The more help I provided of this type to these clients, the more I grew in confidence, and the more people heard about me in the context of my Unique Referral Point. As a Business Coach, I am one of many thousands who are seeking to help others with their organisational, team, or personal development. I can confidently say that in my own neighbourhood and network, enough people know of me as the guy who wants to talk to charities, and they have enough stories of how I have helped them, that I am regularly presented with opportunities to talk with the people I want to talk to. Even better, when I make contact, there is no expectation that I am going to do any particular thing. There is just a shared knowledge of the story used when the introduction was made. If this story was of how I helped someone who had similar needs, the prospective client will be interested to find out if I can help them too. Then, our first conversation will be one in which we are both interested to find out about each other. If a project opportunity emerges, we will be able to co-create it.

A growing area of corporate identity is in the management of Corporate

Reputations. There are many corporations that have a fantastic reputation, and many that don't, so how can we apply the story-telling principles to help us to create and maintain an excellent reputation as our businesses grow?

At micro-business level, one of the keys is to ensure that our associates share our values. Prior to recruiting staff, it is helpful to have trusted associates that you can refer to when the opportunity arises. In looking for trusted associates, we apply the same principles that we are applying to ourselves and our own businesses. We need to get to know them professionally, learn their stories, and when we spot a need, we can make an introduction and back it up with a relevant story. We should only ever introduce people we know and trust though, as our reputation goes with every referral we make. The good news is that we can apply the principles of stories and reputation to develop a network of trusted associates, so let's look at that in more detail.

First thing is to listen out for people who provide the services your customers might need to help you deliver their outcomes. If there are lots of them, ask around for the people your network would recommend. When they make a recommendation, get them to tell you a story. If the story chimes with your core values, there is an opportunity to follow up the introduction and have a conversation with them.

In the conversation, ask them to tell you some stories of people they have helped and how they have helped them. You may even be able to explore their Unique Referral Point with them!

As your network grows, you should keep in touch with them and make sure you keep up to date with their stories. In that way, you will always be able to find them opportunities when help is needed, and if they are working the same way as you, they will be finding opportunities for you. As you may have noticed from my biography, I am a proud member of Business Networks International and BNI® is a great organisation to seek out as all members are encouraged to work in this way. Sharing good news stories about others enhances their reputation, and enhances your reputation too.

It is essential to keep up to date with their stories, and to find ways of keeping in touch. Regular coffees or phone calls (video calls if possible) will help with this, as will keeping up with social media postings. When you talk, make sure you ask them to tell you stories about people they have helped recently and the differences they made. These are the stories that will help you to help them by finding them referrals.

One of the best ways of keeping in touch is of course to pass a referral. I have clients I have helped to whom I regularly pass referrals, and who regularly refer me. They don't need to be colleagues in BNI®, nor do I expect that every referral I pass will result in a referral in return. Simply by passing enough referrals where the needs arise, I know that enough people will be looking out for me and referring me when they spot a need.

Should you get to the stage where you are employing staff, or if you are an employee or team manager, again it is vital to establish that core values are aligned and are supportive of the differences you wish to make. For me this is a way of testing the valuable maxim that 'attitude trumps aptitude'. You can train someone in the skills to do the tasks you want, however you will struggle to change someone's attitude to match yours. Spend some time with them exploring their stories, and see if they chime with your own. When you take references, ask the referees to tell you a story, and especially a story of how the candidate has helped someone recently. It will soon become apparent if your applicant has core values that they live and breathe, and indeed what they are.

This approach applies to larger organisations, and indeed some of the most famous global brands have spent time and money promoting and marketing their values. Famously, in the 1990's when Apple had lost their way, Steve Jobs' directed the marketing team to produce TV advertising that was solely about Apple's core values. They produced a set of advertisements that did not mention their products at all. They simply broadcast people being true to their principles and then added discrete Apple branding. Steve Jobs credits this campaign with the start of the turnaround of Apple Inc.

So the takeaways from this chapter are that it is possible to create a reputation that enhances your business opportunity by being true to your core values, and sticking with them over a long time and throughout your network of associates and employees.

ACTION POINTS

List your core values

Write a story about yourself that reflects you being true to your core values

Write a story about someone you know being true to their core values

Outcomes

You will have noticed a common thread running through the chapters preceding this one. For the Unique Referral Point process to work, we need to stop thinking about ourselves in terms of what we do, and start realising and noticing the outcomes we deliver for others.

In 1985, Edward De Bono said this:

'*Problem analysis* is always looking back at what is already there; *design* is always looking forward at what might be created.

We need to design outcomes. I do not even like saying design 'solutions', because this implies that there is a problem. Even when we cannot find a cause, or, after finding it, cannot remove it, we can always attempt to design an outcome.'

For us to successfully find clients and customers, we need to be aware of the outcomes we deliver for other people, and then relentlessly focus on our ability to deliver these.

If you follow the logic of the book so far, I am asking you to be specific in all your activity, to consider how you help others as the starting point for your work, and to seek introductions to the specific people that need your specific help to deliver their specific outcomes while helping the good people you trust in your network to find introductions to the people for whom they in turn can make a difference. Considering this to be the Unique Referral Point is a tool that I hope helps you to define this for yourself and your organisation. Once you have this, then you will start developing a reputation based in the very specific stories that you tell, and that your network tells on your behalf.

In order to make this work in our own minds, we need to do something that will flip your approach. We need to forget about 'what we do' altogether. It simply is not helpful.

We have looked at the difference between telling people what you do and telling people how you help. In the former, we give ourselves a label – accountant, plumber, personal injury solicitor – and that is it. Whoever we are talking to only hears the label and combining that with whatever other impressions they have formed, they will determine a picture of you that will conform with their own experience.

If you consider yourself on the basis of how you help people, this opens the subject to so much more than just your label.

For example, if you are an Accountant, you will successfully help people reduce their tax bills, or your employer to file the appropriate company accounts and management reports, and for this you will be paid. In addition to your technical skill, what else are you bringing of yourself in order to help your clients? Here are a few ideas:

- You may have specialist skills in a particular sector because of your parents' occupation and your upbringing;
- You may have worked in specific sectors and gained relevant experience that boosts your credibility to help people in related organisations;
- Perhaps you have a large network, drawn from professional and social activity, and you bring that with you to every meeting to help your clients;
- You have a supportive family, enabling you to devote flexible time to your clients so you can cope with awkward and urgent demands for your service.

There are so many more characteristics that you could bring to each client – and none of them are included in the label, 'Accountant'.

Indeed, the more you pursue the 'What I Do Label', the harder it is to represent what you do. If you list all the qualifications and professional memberships you have gained in the field of Accountancy (and there are many), it is making it even harder for your clients to know if they need your services.

On the other hand, if you build a bank of stories about specific people in specific sectors whose tax bill you have reduced, you will be presented by your network as a useful person, and they will be able to refer to you.

Consider the plumber for instance. Virtually all of us have at some point had some work completed in our homes. And, virtually all of us at some point have had a neighbour asking if we would recommend the trades-person when they need something similar in their home.

When we make the recommendation of our plumber, what do we talk about? If you are happy to recommend them, chances are that they were neat and tidy, punctual, polite, minimised disruption, and finished the job early or on time, and within budget. Combine any of these and you will find they feature in your story about your plumber.

At any stage, did you ask the plumber about the wrenches they were using? The materials? The specific order of installation of the bathroom suite? How a close-coupled cistern mechanism works? No – because (a) you expected them to have this knowledge and to be able to apply it, and (b) you don't have the knowledge to hold a balanced conversation on these topics, so unless you simply wanted to learn for your own benefit, there was no need to ask. The discussions are instead all focused on the outcomes. What is the purpose of the bathroom? (Yes – there is the obvious, however it may be important to know if this bathroom is for children, or elderly, or requires special adaptation for disability.) What is the theme? Favourite colours? The tiles, wall coverings, lighting, sound system or TV requirements? The list of characteristics are all desired outcomes the customer wants after the job has been done. If this happens naturally in the bathroom installation market, how come we spend so much time asking (and answering) the question, 'How Much?' before any party has discussed the desired outcomes?

Now, let's move on to the next level of outcomes as a means of securing a referral.

In conversation with your plumber, let's imagine you asked about their family, and found out that they had values similar to yours. Perhaps they were working hard to fund their children's education, or to meet the particular needs of their elderly parents. In their spare time, maybe they volunteer their services to support a local charity, or to coach the kids' football team. None of these are anything to do with plumbing, however all of them are credibility enhancing reasons to support a recommendation to a neighbour. You can imagine the conversation including one of these elements as the additional information reinforces the confidence of the referrer that the plumber they are referring is someone they can refer with confidence. This extra level of helpful information increases the likelihood that the neighbour will get in touch, and also that they will be pleased with the outcomes the plumber can deliver. This is useful in a professional context as well. For example, if the plumber has completed work in particularly challenging houses, perhaps where the property was old and there were tricky obstacles to overcome, it is likely that this story would be helpful in securing a referral. If the plumber has shared this story with their network, this will enhance their reputation. If the story fits their URP, this will also help them to find more referrals.

The outcomes are all important, and my third example illustrates this perfectly.

My friend Mike is a Personal Injury Solicitor. He specialises in supporting the victims of rape and sexual assault, securing the compensation *to which victims are entitled* from the Criminal Injuries' Compensation Board. In conversation with Mike, I asked him to tell me more about some of the people he had helped recently. He told me of one client who had been assaulted when a teenager. Her parents had settled on her behalf, and when Mike reviewed her case, the amount they had received had been a lot less then her entitlement. Mike pursued her case, it was reopened, and thanks to his help, they secured an amount of money (*her entitlement – remember!*) that enabled her to rebuild and move on with her life through being able to move into her own home, go back to University to study, and to start a new career.

What a wonderful set of outcomes to be able to deliver!

So, with this kind of story, you would think that groups supporting rape and sexual assault victims would be keen to hear from Mike and his colleagues, and keen to invite them to support the people they in turn are supporting. Sadly, not a bit of it.

Thanks to his label of 'Personal Injury Solicitor', he has been called many and various things. The politest is probably, 'Ambulance Chaser', and he has been told on many occasions that he is profiting on other people's misery. He cannot get an invitation to attend support group meetings, let alone to speak at them, and certainly never to be passed as a useful contact to the support group's clients.

This disconnect occurs simply because of the 'What I Do' label, and the gap that exists between the label and the whole person. If you let them, your clients and customers will fill in that gap. If what you do is well received and well known, or simple to understand and relate to, you probably won't need to worry as your Profession's reputation enhances your credibility. On the other hand, if your label has negative connotations, no matter how unfair or undeserved, following the URP process and focusing on the outcomes you deliver will help you to educate your network and your prospective clients and customers to the real difference you make as a rounded human being with specific technical skills in one area.

Before I go any further, I need to expand on 'Outcomes' as there are specific characteristics to defining and developing your outcomes focused approach.

As Edward de Bono said, it is a limiting approach to think that we can only offer outcomes that tackle problems. To open up the conversation, rather than talking about solutions, problems or opportunities, let us simply refer to the client having a Goal. And note, the Goal could be the 'solving' of a problem, or it could be the achievement of something positive. The essential step we need to take is to convert the Goal into a set of parameters that we can work towards, and that we can notice happening as we make progress.

Here are the key elements that must go into an Outcome for it to qualify:

1. The outcome sought must be Specific;
2. When the outcome is achieved, there will be Observable differences;
3. If these differences are to be Observable, they will also be Measurable;
4. None of us live in unique isolation, so there will be Interactional elements;
5. To help root the outcomes, they will need to be related to a point in Time.

Let me give you a simple example.

A client presents their goal as, 'I want to be happy'.

The traditional, expert advice approach would be to help the client be happy by drawing on the expert's own experience of happiness, and to offer advice about how the client could 'do' things that will 'make them happy'. (Forgive me – this is a deliberately simple example!). Typically, helpful suggestions will be made, and the hope is that some of the suggestions will resonate with the client in a way that helps them to be happy.

To help us to develop stories in our network about how we have helped people, the stories need to concern Specific, Observable, Measurable, Interactional, Time-related Outcomes.

Let's look back at the situation facing Mike. He has tried approaching support groups, however he gets the cold shoulder and so doesn't make much progress. Yet he delivers life changing outcomes for the people receiving support from the support group. What if he was to promote himself using the outcomes first?

Imagine you were running a support group, and you received a recommendation from a friend that you needed to talk to Mike as he can help the support group clients. Naturally, you would ask what Mike does, and instead of being told his label, you were told the following, 'Well, first he's a really nice guy, and the main thing is I know that he helped someone recently to move into their own house, go back to University to study, and to rebuild their lives.' Naturally you would ask, 'So how did he do that?', and at that point, our helpful referrer could say what Mike does, knowing that the support group organiser is thinking about the people they are supporting who would benefit from moving house, retraining, and rebuilding their lives.

This is an approach you can apply to all business development activity. Take a moment to define the Outcomes you deliver for others, and list them.

Now, pick one of these and consider the difference your clients notice as a result of you helping them to reach their outcome. If you sell products, what is the difference your clients notice after they have purchased your product.

Who else is involved in this? What do they notice? It is sometimes easier to think about others who are involved rather than think about ourselves. For example, when we are happy, we may see others smiling at us. Interactional events that we notice tell us that our desired difference is happening. If we look for it and notice it when it happens, we know we are making progress.

Now, for each of the above Outcomes, list the SOMIT elements that turn these into noticeable differences on a table like this:

Outcome	
Specific	
Observable	
Measurable	
Interactional	
Time-related	

Here are questions you can ask to help you:

Thinking about a client who realises Outcome (x):

- Can I describe the client Outcome from my perspective as provider in language which is specific, starting with 'I help...' or 'help to...';
- If the outcome is achieved, what differences will my client notice?
- Can I/we/they measure this noticeable difference? If so, what is my/our/their method of measurement (could simply be to notice it happening);
- Who else is involved? What differences will they notice?
- When will I/we/they notice these differences?

Let's look back a few pages to the plumber and new bathroom example. All the Outcomes listed fit the SOMIT model. Before the plumber can begin the work, they need to know the purpose of the bathroom, the people it is to be used by, the colours and materials, the equipment, and of course the final stage will be planning in the work to a schedule. With this full set of specific, observable, measurable, interactional and time related differences to work towards, the plumber has a specification and knows that delivering this specification for an agreed price will likely lead to a happy customer, and ultimately to more recommendations and referrals.

Focusing on the Outcomes you deliver gives you huge opportunity to bring your whole self to the process of finding people to help, and of helping more people. We are all so much more than our technical skill set and our qualifications. Once you have brought these strands together, you will benefit from word of mouth referrals from your network that are the ones you actually want, and that have a high probability of being an opportunity to help someone to achieve their desired outcomes, and an opportunity to do business.

Outcomes Focused Marketing

Most businesses have many ways of promoting their business. At the start of our business life, we will nearly all invest in basic information provision about our business. After all, if we don't tell the world we have arrived, how will they know? To this end, most businesses spend start-up finance on a combination of business cards, leaflets, a website, brochures, social media pages and profiles, and maybe a liveried vehicle if appropriate to our profession.

And most businesses spend a lot of time filling these promotional spaces with a long list of 'things I do'.

There is an opportunity to apply the techniques I have outlined in this book and to revise the materials you use to promote yourself on the basis of the outcomes you provide and the people you want to help achieve those outcomes.

Instead of promoting yourself and talking about the things you do, it is helpful to develop specific phrases that start with, 'I help', mention, 'specific people', and finish with, 'outcomes'. You will hopefully have developed your own Unique Referral Point which will make it easier to determine which of the many promotion methods will be the most appropriate to deliver your outcomes focused message to your target clients. And you will also be thinking about stories you can tell that support your activities and that enhance your credibility.

The easiest way to do this is to consider your materials with an outcomes focussed approach.

Here are the stages you could go through to make this an efficient process:

1. Which of your many routes of information and story sharing (media, social media, networking etc) are shared with your target clients or customers?

2. Having identified these, revise the information shared so that it describes your top outcomes delivered, differences made and your favourite types of clients you wish to help.

3. Remove all lengthy descriptions of the things you do.

4. Replace with stories of people you have helped and how you helped them. Case studies are great, and will complement any testimonials received.

5. Ruthlessly apply the 80/20 rule until you reduce your offer to a manageable list of specialist Unique Referral Points.

6. If you have too many pages on your website, or you scroll for ages on your social media profiles, look to edit and reduce so that you provide interesting stories that encourage people with similar needs to get in touch and ask you for more.

In many respects, this is an art form, and you won't necessarily get the changes spot on first time around. However, the easiest way I can illustrate the idea is to compare it to the dating process; finding a partner, possibly for life.

If you are dating now, I hope this is useful, and if it is a distant memory, I hope this chimes with your own experiences. When you meet someone you are attracted to, what happens if you engage them with a full list of the things you would like to do with them for the rest of your lives together? You know, marriage, family, mortgage, etc. Does that work on the first approach? No, of course not. So why do we lay out our full package of services on our promotional materials? I am no expert in dating however here are some thoughts around development of relationships.

In order to develop an initial attraction into a long-term relationship that delivers all of the desired for outcomes, the process must be of mutual interest. Both parties need to show interest – and therefore there needs to be some mystery so that relevant questions can be asked and information shared. If compatibility and mutual attraction is established, a next small step might be to meet for coffee and to share more information and ask more questions, developing the relationship. Only after going on a number of dates and progressing at a mutually compatible pace will a new relationship be formed.

It is a similar process when a prospective client is looking for a product or service. However they find you, they will need to know just enough information to be attracted to you to the point where they get in touch. It may be that your enquiry is simple (e.g. booking a camp site for a holiday) in which case the response is simple. However, if your services are complex, you answer the questions posed by your enquirer and perhaps you ask some of your own. In this way, early compatibility is established, and if appropriate, meeting up might be proposed to discuss the needs of the client further. You will see later how this can then be transformed into business opportunity. For now, take the Outcomes Focus and apply it to your conversations and your promotional materials. I hope this has a transformational effect.

ACTION POINTS

Think of a recent occasion when you helped someone. Can you define the Specific, Observable, Measurable and Interactional differences you and they noticed, and over what Time-scale?

List here the Outcomes you have delivered for clients recently:

Who else needs these? List them here:

If needs be, continue this list on a separate piece of paper...

Networking

Networking! Does your heart sink when you contemplate the need to network? Have you *ever* had a good networking experience? Networking has a poor reputation as a way of generating business opportunity, and there is one simple reason for this. No one likes being sold to – and most people go networking to find people they can sell to. If you are in a room full of people who want to sell, no-one is thinking of the needs they have, and so there is no-one minded to buy. As a result, most networking is considered unproductive, even by enthusiastic participants. And yet…

On an informal basis, we all have a network which generates word of mouth referrals. When you need something for your home, it is common to ask your neighbours for a recommendation. What results is a word of mouth referral. When you go to a party and the food is excellent, you ask the host who the caterer was. Result? Another word of mouth referral will follow when the Occasion presents itself. If your network is generating word of mouth referrals for you, then that is your network working.

How Networking 'Works'

For a start, we need to address the 'selling to the network' approach. No-one likes being sold to, so whatever line of business you are in, think hard about how you are presenting yourself. True Net 'working' happens when you and your network are making connections, and the natural need for a connection arises when someone needs some help. If you know someone who can provide that help, you make the connection there and then. Most of us want to help people where there is a need. Recognise this exchange?

- *'Hi, could you do me a favour?'*
- *'Yes of course, what is it?'*

When asked by someone to do them a favour, we say, 'yes' before we know what the favour is! Good networkers are always looking for opportunities to match those who need help with those who can provide the help by making an introduction. The Net 'working' process starts this way round, so don't go asking your network for business. Work on your natural tendencies to help others, and you will start feeling the benefits in time.

Developing Useful Introductions

When someone needs help, we will help them ourselves or introduce someone who can help. Everyone can do this already at a basic level. For example, if someone is ill, we would recommend a trusted Doctor – the label is enough on this occasion. If you are wishing to grow the professional network of supporters you can call on when someone you know has a need, it is useful to find out how they in turn help people. I have one very simple question that gives me this information rapidly and memorably:

'Please tell me a story about how you helped someone recently?'

I use this question when I am getting to know people, so this is very appropriate in a professional context or when networking. This also accelerates the process of finding referrals.

For example, previously we met the Heating Engineer called P, and I asked the question above. He told me that he had recently helped a Printing Company to stabilise the environment in their warehouse, helping them to print more efficiently. I asked him how this had helped the printers with that outcome, and P told me that temperature and humidity are critical to the printing process and need to be precisely controlled. P was able to do this, saving the printer time, and reducing their waste so saving them money and ultimately making them more profitable.

It is now very easy for me to refer printers to P, and in addition, for any building I walk into where there is a need (or an obvious failure) to control the environment for the comfort and productivity of the people and the operation.

The URP Pyramid and The Referrals Process

In looking at our URP, we have already worked through the principles of the URP Pyramid in terms of improving our own practice. By following this process, we also improve the chances of us receiving the referrals we want to that will help us to keep working within our chosen URPs.

Within our networks, we all have people we recommend. At a simple level, this is based on our own experience, so for example, if the plumber did a great job fitting our bathroom, we will recommend them to neighbours needing a new bathroom. We might only know one plumber, and it is highly likely they were recommended to us originally.

When we are looking to make a referral, the higher up the URP pyramid our contact is, the more likely we are to refer them.

When we start practicing, we are a Novice, and very few people will refer to a novice. Often, we are one of many in our field, and there are many who never move beyond this level, however through practicing for a period of time, they manage to sustain themselves and do OK. Successful novices will make a living, and as their stories develop, and their clients start recommending them, they move to Practitioner. More referrals will come, and for most people in any market sector, this is the area where they will spend the bulk of their career. For some Practitioners, they have a particular skill, or desire to share their skills with other Practitioners, and these people become Experts. Now think about introducing someone from your network to a friend who needs help. It is more likely that we will recommend an expert in something than a mere practitioner, so moving up the pyramid helps increase your referrals, and hopefully your network will refer for the things in which you are an Expert.

Moving on from Expert, I consider the next level to be that of Influencer. This could include the modern, social media Influencer who by dint of their follower base can be hired to promote a brand message, however that type of Influencer appears to be created more by good fortune than by any real expertise. More practically, and within our own control, Influencer level is where an Expert starts helping others. Helping others to learn from you by whatever means will help you become an Influencer, and this is a natural progression for many who are Expert in their field. Influencers are likely to have more stories about helping others, and so therefore are more likely to receive high quality referrals. They may also have published their Influential thoughts and ideas in ways which enable them to reach (and so to Influence) people beyond their own capacity. As well as the traditional book-publishing, there are many ways of delivering this level of influence on-line, however only a few will successfully influence a large network beyond their capacity. At this level, your network will really start to work for you as your story is in the public domain, and will be shared by people you don't know and have never met. It is easy to refer an Influencer, and their story is available in published or on-line form! It is also a massive credibility boost for me as the referrer if I am able to recommend an Influencer that I know, trust and refer to regularly.

Then, at the top of the pyramid, and usually occupying the solitary chair, is the Guru. This is the person known universally as the ultimate practitioner, expert, influencer in their field. We can all think of examples in the public domain, and in large pyramids, there may be more than one who can claim Guru status. At this level, people will pay handsomely for half an hour of the Guru's time. Long term maintenance of Guru status is as much down to reputation management as it is to the progress through the levels of the pyramid. When thinking of referring to the Guru, we all think twice. We need to make sure that our reputation is not reduced in the eyes of the Guru so we can maintain our ability to refer to them, therefore we will only refer the opportunities we know they are likely to want. A successful referral to a Guru makes us look great in the eyes of the person we are helping, as long as the match is a good one for all involved. The URP Process applies as you pass referrals within your pyramid too.

Gurus and Influencers will be referred by all, however not all the referrals will be personal. For example, a novice may be recommended to read an Influencer's book, or attend a conference where the Guru is giving a plenary talk. It is hard for the novice to find a referral to a third party where there is a genuine need for the Guru's level of expertise in person. However, a novice can easily refer an expert when they are not confident that they have the skills to help. The more experts the novice knows, the more they will learn, and the better referrals they will pass. The final part of the URP pyramid is this process of passing referrals to the next level up the pyramid, in combination with the skills enhancement, experience, client stories, credibility and reputation.

So in addition to finding referrals for and learning from those above you in your technical skill-set, how do you climb the pyramid and elevate yourself from Novice so that you can receive the referrals that will help you to grow and climb the URP ladder?

Well, there are two approaches. For P, our Plumber, he can try to become the Guru of Plumbers. This will involve a lot of work, and will take time, however there is always a Guru and it could just as easily be P.

Alternatively, P can find a smaller, more specific Pyramid, and start developing his Guru status there.

Thinking about their Unique Referral Point, P has a simple answer to the question, 'So what do you do?'. He can say:

- *'I help printing companies make more money by precisely regulating their print environment, reducing waste and increasing productivity.'*

If P chooses to define his URP as wishing to help more printers with the above outcomes, his pyramid is immediately made smaller as he is only looking to be the Climate Control Guru to the Print Industry.

For a start, there will be less Practitioners focussing on this sector. He has already demonstrated his credibility, so has made Expert status simply by delivering this benefit to one client already. In this example, there may be little need for the Influencing level, though I am sure he would be welcome at a Print Industry convention if his talk was entitled, 'Reducing Waste and Increasing Productivity in the Print Process', so this is an easy stage for him to progress towards. If the Print Industry trade press picks up on his convention talk, and he develops the theme through further talks, blog posts, training, and through sharing good stories on-line or through writing technical articles or even a book sharing the message of the importance of this aspect of printing, eventually, the print industry will recognise P as the Guru in this very specific market sector, and P will have the ideal Unique Referral Point position.

The Networking System

Let's look at this as a practical system that you can apply to your own situation.

To generate word of mouth referrals for your organisation, you need a large network of people that you keep in touch with regularly, and that through this you get to know them and trust them. In keeping in touch, you learn their stories, and in particular the stories of how they have helped people. By the same process, they learn your stories, and the stories of how you have helped people. Then, when you (and they) are going about their daily work, or socialising, or chatting with strangers in the bus queue, if a need is spotted where someone needs help, it should be possible to introduce someone you know and trust to provide that help. This is a referral – and you need to give referrals to your network as often as you can. If you are giving to your network, they will find and give referrals to you.

When I started my coaching career, it was as a BizFizz Coach in Bradford, a city in Yorkshire in the North of England. Bradford was a part of the great textiles trade that blossomed from the Industrial Revolution onwards until as late as after the Second World War. At one stage, Bradford was the terminus for three railway companies, had canals to the North and South, and had so many mills producing that it was once the 'wool capital of the world'. As the textiles industry declined in the later 20th century, so the city has faced many challenges. I started my coaching career helping people start businesses in two areas of the city that were in the poorest 10% of areas in Europe for economic performance.

At the time, Bradford was running many projects where the offer was made of business advice and support, and the engagement process involved marketing, leaflets, events, posters, and lots of people in power dress inviting clients to visit them in their city centre offices. This was common across the UK, and I am sure is common where you are. BizFizz was radically different.

BizFizz was founded by the New Economics Foundation and the Civic Trust as a research project that set out to test the hypothesis that a pure coaching approach would be more successful in helping entrepreneurs start and grow businesses. This required the support of the local community, and so the project model was designed as follows.

The local coach was recruited by and then supervised by the Local Management Group, all of whom were drawn from the local community. Once appointed, the first task of the BizFizz Coach was to meet with people for 1-2-1 coffees to find out more about them, and to tell them about the project. The offer was that if they knew anyone who was interested in starting a business, or in developing their existing business, they were to give that person one of the Coach's business cards and ask them to get in touch. Two things were key about this process. First, there was no marketing – all we had was a pack of business cards. Second, the prospective client had to phone the coach. This was important as it set the balance from the start that the client was in control of their own journey.

In these 1-2-1 meetings, there were other possible outcomes. The local person might think of others who would be useful for the coach to meet, and then make an introduction. Or, they might become keen to support in which case they would be invited to help clients by joining the local Panel meeting. The local panel would meet to answer questions clients had asked the coach. The coach would present these entirely free of context so that the Panel only offered the advice sought, and did not voice opinions on other topics. The coach would record and anonymise all the answers and feed back to the client, and so the pure coaching model was maintained.

At every stage of this process, referrals are being generated. In addition, as the programme gained clients, so the local networking would result in referrals for the clients. Not surprisingly, local people want to use local businesses, and so the coach became a focal point for referral requests when people had a need.

Having been a BizFizz Coach for a couple of years, I was lucky enough to join BNI®, Business Network International®. BNI® has taken the process of generating word of mouth referrals and formalised it, developing it into a very impressive and successful system of generating word of mouth referrals, and I am proud to have been a member since 2009. As a BizFizz Coach in Bradford operating on a networking project that generated word of mouth referrals, I was properly at home, and I have given myself wholeheartedly to learning, developing and following the system in all I do. In my opinion, there are two reasons to become a member of BNI®: to learn the system properly; to grow the network you are in that works with the same system. Ultimately if you use this system, you will generate word of mouth referrals for your network and by extension, yourself.

The Key Elements of the Networking System

The way I have organised this book has been to introduce the key elements of the system in the order you need them. Here are the elements combined in explanation:

1. Being Specific
2. Knowing how you help others
3. Being passionate about what you do
4. Knowing your URP
5. Focusing on the Outcomes
6. Telling and Learning Stories
7. Making Connections

Combining all of these into your networking activity will result in word of mouth referrals. Let's work through the system in order.

1. Being Specific

From the very start of your networking activity, it is essential that you are specific in your description of yourself. You will know the reasons why having read this far. When seeking referrals, the more specific you are about your products and services, the easier it is to refer you. For example, if a friend needs a plumber to service their oil-fired boiler in their thatched cottage in a rural part of the countryside, chances are that a referral to someone with specialist knowledge of their circumstances, backed up with a good story of how they have helped someone similar will be a good referral for your friend. It is unlikely you will have confidence in a general handyman who does a bit of plumbing for them to be referred on this occasion.

2. Knowing how others help, and how you help others

To receive referrals, first you need to give them. BNI® has researched this, and their advice is that for every qualified referral you wish to receive, you need to be giving at least two qualified referrals to your network. To do this, you need to find out about how others help, so ask them to tell you a story about how they have helped someone recently. Similarly, when you are asked what you do, answer with how you help. If further explanation is needed, give a relevant and recent example.

Unless your service is clear from the label attached, your network needs to know how you help people, and who you help. For the last five years, I have been promoting myself to my network as being interested in helping Charities with sustainable revenue generation. As a result, I receive regular referrals to Charities who need help with this important aspect of their operation. My network doesn't even need to know how I help – they just know that I have credibility, and that I have helped other charities. That is enough for them to refer me.

3. Being passionate about what you do

Your passion will come across in all you do. Conversely, if you are not passionate, that will be obvious also. If you are not passionate about what you do, and the help you are providing, then think again. Remember, your network needs to have total confidence in you to make a referral on your behalf. Passion is the vital ingredient that enhances and supports every referral and the corresponding story.

4. Knowing your URP

When I talk about the charities I want to help, they are all local to me, and the largest operate on a regional basis. When I talk about the entrepreneurs I help, they are all pre-start, start-up or micro businesses. I have credibility and lots of great stories of helping people in these sectors, so I am very happy when a referral is made to someone who fits one of these (or both of these) groups. This also enables me to pass referrals on to others where the client or the specific need are not within my URP profile. And if I am passing referrals to people who are similar to me in the things they do, it is natural that they will find clients for me and return the favour.

5. Focusing on the Outcomes

It is essential that your network knows about the Outcomes you deliver for others as this will help identify the needs and will create the opportunity for an introduction. If you are promoting yourself through marketing or on-line, the outcomes you deliver will be the most interesting aspect of your communication to others. When you are talking with people about how you helped others, or finding out about the help they need, the outcomes are the only thing to be looking for. If someone needs help to achieve them, you will know someone who can help.

6. Telling and Learning Stories

The human condition is to tell stories. The wonderful thing about this system of connecting people through giving and receiving referrals is that we are all fantastic at telling stories when we receive the merest trigger to our memories.

Take a moment to think of the last conversation you had that involved telling a story. Now consider a couple of things. Did you tell the story in a word for word repetition of the last time you told the story? Or word for word repetition of the way you heard the story? No, of course not. Our brains store away key details and then we improvise the story to suit the occasion and the audience. Indeed with this in mind, we will tell the same story in different ways, and with greater or lesser levels of embellishment depending on the circumstances.

7. Making Connections

A network is an active, interconnected group of people, and we all have our own unique network already. If you follow the process outlined so far, you will naturally spot people who need the help of others, and you will be able to make a connection to someone who can help. When the person needing help asks you, 'so what do they do?', you will be able to tell a story about the way they have helped someone who was in a similar situation. This is massively more powerful than introducing someone by their Label as it works on many more occasions, especially where the Label does not accurately represent the whole person. The most important aspect of this introduction method is that the less you discuss what your network partner can do for the person with the need, the easier it is for the conversation between them to be productive.

When I am introduced to people, I really don't want my network to have told them what I do, how I do it, the challenges I will overcome, or worst of all, how much I will charge! If the conversation moves onto, 'so what does he do?', I am very happy for my network partner to politely decline to explain, and suggest that I am the best person to talk with. At that point, the introduction is made, and I will become involved at the start of the conversation, rather than needing to unpick all the elements of the conversation that was held in my absence.

If you have mastered the seven elements above, you are ready to start having URP and Outcomes Focused conversations with people, and this will start to get your network working.

Natural Conversations

Networking takes many forms. We are all familiar with the formal networking event, however whenever you meet someone, if you are tuned in to the help they might need, then this is a networking opportunity.

I often meet people starting out in business who worry about the isolation of their situation. They describe themselves as lonely or bored, missing the company of others, and on occasion they give up their dream of self-employment and go back to being employed, sacrificing one set of freedoms for the opportunity to be part of a work based social network. And yet, these same people will be buying groceries, receiving post, having the bins emptied, chatting with neighbours, meeting parents at the school gate, or chatting with fellow dog-walkers. And the only time they think they can talk about business is when they are in a room full of other business people who are all trying to sell to them! No wonder many give up on their dreams.

I often hear people, both employed and self-employed, saying that they don't want to talk about work. Yet 'work' is at the heart of what we do most days, and if it was our favourite hobby, we would talk about it for hours.

If you take the URP system I have described to heart, every conversation becomes an opportunity to talk about your passion, your ability to help someone else, either through your own work, or often by making an introduction to people who are similarly passionate about what they do and the people they help.

The good news is that with practice, this becomes an extension of your normal conversations. Remember the last time you recommended your plumber to a neighbour? If you told a story about how good they were to reinforce the referral, then all you need to do is to learn more stories about more people that you get to know and trust, and the opportunity to help will grow.

The Easy Opportunity

So with so much opportunity, where shall we begin? Well, let's look at our existing network first.

Unless you are living on a desert island, you are connected with some people. These could be friends, family, neighbours, fellow parents, dog walkers, or if you are already trading, these are clients, suppliers, people you meet at events, and many others besides. Let's not worry about the more random strangers for now – we can start with the strangers we know.

It is a perfectly natural conversation to ask someone how work is going, or how their business is doing. We do this all the time, and it is a polite and acceptable conversation. So what would your reaction be if a client called you up and said something like this:

'Hi, I was wondering if we could meet for coffee. I would like to find out more about your business and see if I can help you with some referrals. Would that be ok?'

Imagine receiving that call. What's the worst that could happen? Of course you are going to accept the invitation.

Now, let's swap roles. If you have a supplier, what would their reaction be if you rang them up and asked them to meet for a coffee so you can find out more about their business and see if you can find them some referrals? Wouldn't that be amazing? And of course, it would be perfectly natural in that coffee conversation for you to make sure that time was taken for them to find out about your business and see if they could find you referrals too.

The great outcome of this process is that more referrals will help each of you to be more secure and successful in your businesses, and so more likely to be able to continue to support each other in the long term.

If you have clients, ask yourself, 'When was the last time I passed a referral to one of my clients?' I pass referrals to my clients regularly, after all I know them well and I have great stories from my work with them. I often refer a client to another client. For all the value I add, if I can make a referral to them that helps them grow their business, that is adding extra value above and beyond, and helping me to cement my relationship with my client in the process.

The process is identical with your suppliers. If they haven't read this book yet and already called you, give them a call. If you value your supplier, help them grow their business. As well as raising your profile with your supplier, this will help them to find referrals for you as they learn about your business and the specific help you can provide to a specific set of other people. It is highly likely that they know some people like the ones you want to help, and they probably didn't realise you wanted to help them. How great will they look to their suppliers and clients if they are making high quality referral introductions on a regular basis?

In these conversations, there are some key things I would recommend.

The first is not to spend too much time sharing what you do. Remember that your label won't win business on its own, and nor will lengthy tales of your processes and activities. Instead, ask for some stories of how the other person has helped others recently, and then ask questions about the stories they tell to get more detail that is relevant about them as a whole person.

The second is to find out if they are looking for referrals to more people like those they have described helping in the stories they have just shared with you. If so, you can perhaps think of people you could introduce them to. If not, ask them to tell you another story about how they have helped someone where they enjoyed it so much themselves that they would like the chance to help others in a similar way.

The third part of the conversation is to make sure you ask them what challenges they are facing at the moment. Maybe there will be none, however it is likely that whoever you are talking to will have some challenges, and in the spirit of following the system, you might be able to make a qualified referral to someone who can help them overcome their current challenge. There is a risk at this point that the other person will mention a challenge with which you could help them directly. Yet that wasn't the reason you asked to see them – so what do you do? There is no right or wrong answer here, however unless they are stating that they need immediate help and you are the very person to help them, I would recommend you park that need until you have explored the conversation properly, and then maybe come back to that at the end. Personally, I would always look to set up another conversation to discuss this need properly when both they and you are in the frame of mind to start shaping a project specification. That will preserve your networking activity as just that, and not lead to people thinking you are selling by surreptitious means.

The fourth is to make sure that you are both aware of the outcomes you want from this meeting. When setting it up, be explicit that the reason you want to meet is to find out more about their business so you can find them referrals, and that is it. Don't make it a precondition that they are going to ask you the same and find referrals for you as that might not work with everyone. Just be sure that when you meet with them, you have set the parameters so they don't think this is a pretence so that you can get in there to sell to them!

So there is a very easy opportunity to get out there and grow your referral network using the system.

Networking Events

As a proud member of BNI®, I recommend visiting a local group and you will see people applying the system in the way BNI® has developed it, formalising, testing and advancing the system of generating word of mouth referrals for each other.

If you attend a BNI® meeting, or any other event, you will meet interesting people. This is where using this system enables you to develop your network, however don't expect it to happen in the meeting itself. If you have a productive conversation in the meeting, it is likely to be short, however if there is mutual opportunity, or if the person is someone you think you could refer, ask them for a coffee to make time to go through the process outlined above. The more of these opportunities you have for coffees, the better a network you will build and the more useful you will be when making introductions when you spot a need.

Now I know that there are many networking organisations who compare themselves to BNI®, and describe the pressure to bring a referral to each weekly meeting. There are also some members I have met who act in a similar way, and feel the pressure. I prefer to flip this entirely on its head. While I have mentioned BNI® and I have learned a lot from being a member, if you just applied this system to your BNI® colleagues (or the colleagues in any other networking group) and you didn't apply it to the rest of your network, you are simply reducing your opportunity to help and be helped.

The way I describe my networking activity to others is that I have a large network of people that I keep in touch with regularly. I learn their stories, and share mine with them, and through this process when I find someone who has a need, I hope to make an introduction. I follow that introduction up with an email to both parties, and I will always call the person I am referring after the conversation where their help was identified. In this way, I can share the story that lead to the referral, and the story I told to reinforce the credibility of the person I was referring to. Now, here's the thing. I apply this with my whole network of trusted people. I therefore pass 8-10 referrals per week, sometimes more. Of these, some will be to members of BNI®, and of these, some will be to colleagues in my BNI® group.

The good news is that by following the process in this book, you can make this work for you. I highly recommend that if you want to learn and practice the system with like-minded entrepreneurial colleagues, find and join your local BNI® group. If you already think you know the system, however you would like a larger network to refer to and receive referrals from, again find and join your local BNI® group. The key aspect is that however you do it, you need to be giving to your network in the form of your time, your conversation, your learning of their stories, and when appropriate the passing of referrals. Do this often, and your network will work for you.

ACTION POINTS

List three clients and three suppliers you are confident you could refer to.

CLIENTS   SUPPLIERS

1.   1.

2.   2.

3.   3.

Contact them to book a coffee to find out more about their stories of how they have helped others. See if you can then find them referrals to similar people with similar needs.

Referral Conversion

I am guessing that unless you are brand new in business, you will have received some referrals already, or some enquiries generated from your marketing or on-line activities. If so, what is your conversion rate from initial enquiry through to closed business? In this chapter we will look at applying the system in this book and the process that significantly increases your conversion rate and ensures that you deliver in a way that minimises your stress levels and makes you money.

Receiving a Referral

One of the things I often ask my pre-start clients is, 'What are you going to do when the client says yes?', as believe it or not, many new entrepreneurs don't think through this scenario. By a similar token what are you going to do when you receive a referral?

For most of us, first point of contact would be the prospective client, however that approach misses out some valuable steps that are helpful if followed.

Since the URP process will generate referrals, it is helpful if we know how the process was applied. So here are some steps to take when receiving a referral.

First, contact the member of your network who has made the introduction. Find out the specific story of how the introduction was made, and don't scrimp on the details. You should find out as much as possible, including the relationship between your network member and the prospective client, the need identified, the conversation that identified the need, and what your network member has said to introduce you.

If your network partner has referred you due to the prospective client having a need for some outcomes, and they have told a story of how you have delivered similar outcomes elsewhere, this is a good start to your conversation. It is highly likely though that your referral partner may have said something else. For example, they may have mentioned your label, the things you do, or passed some other comment such as, 'He's really helpful – he gave me a massive discount!' It is really useful if you know this information before you contact the prospective client so that you can re-frame the conversation at the start of your referral development process.

Following the URP process will increase the likelihood that you will be referred in a way that increases the likelihood of a successful follow up.

Ideally, you will have been referred due to a need for a specific outcome and this will have been backed up by a relevant story. It is for this reason that I encourage you to work on these – it will massively improve the quality of referrals you receive. If your reputation is of delivering quality outcomes, and is underpinned by many supportive stories, each referral you receive will be a genuine opportunity to co-create an opportunity to help someone. You will be a step closer to your Seven Day Weekend. As you will see from the next stage of converting referrals, the use of Outcomes at the start of this process is essential to the success of this next step. If you receive a referral that is not all about Outcomes, there is work to do to establish these before we can begin to move on beyond the initial referral receipt stage.

This is all very helpful information when you actually approach the prospective client. Is it time to do that now?

If you have obtained more details from the referrer, in the internet age, it is now time to do your own homework. Take a look on-line and review their website, their social media presence, and see if you can develop a picture of some of the challenges they are facing. This will also give you a glimpse of the bigger picture, enhancing the story told by your network member when they introduced you, and enhancing your credibility.

So now you have a good picture of the referral scenario, it is safe to contact them. At this point, pick up the phone.

Yes, pick up the phone.

If you choose any other method of making initial contact, the referral will go nowhere. And by the way, if your network member has not secured the phone number for you and told you it is ok to call, ask them to see if they can do that for you so you can follow up properly!

Making an approach by email will not work when responding to a referral need. The only exception to this is if you have trained your network that you can only respond by email to enquiries due to some restriction in which case the prospect client will be expecting your email. In all other cases, the referral follow up starts with a conversation.

The Phone Call

If you have taken the steps above then the prospective client will be expecting your call, and your credibility is enhanced immediately through your connection with the referrer and your knowledge of the story. Your background research will also enhance your credibility, especially if it enables you to ask some questions relating to the need for which you have been referred.

If in the phone call, you establish the need, the only outcome from the phone call should be a further conversation. If you are in close enough proximity, a face to face meeting over a coffee would be ideal. If that is not an option, a video call would be the next best means of having a meeting. And finally, a scheduled phone call where enough time is allowed for a proper discussion could be your third option.

Now it may be that in the phone call, your prospective customer asks you to send more information. If you haven't established the outcomes, the needs, the differences the customer is seeking, it is virtually impossible at this stage to send any information that will lead to them commissioning you. It may be appropriate if you are offering products and the need is obvious. You could send some information (bearing in mind the information should be outcomes focused if possible), while also seeking dates for a follow up conversation or meeting to review the information you send. In cases where you are offering services, or bespoke products, sending information on its own will reduce your conversion likelihood. Why so? Simply you are leaving it to your client to make the connection between your information and the need. If you have a meeting in the diary, suggest that you will bring information with you to the meeting. If you are struggling to get a meeting, and you have information to hand, send it out of politeness and arrange a follow up phone call with time to discuss the needs in the context of the information. If possible, hold onto the information for now. There are some steps to follow before the right information can be shared.

The further conversation is an essential first point in converting a referral into business. It is this conversation that enables you to go through the stages identified so far in this book. To follow the system, you must approach this with the mindset that you are looking to help this person with a set of outcomes after you have done your thing – and that may be by not providing them with your products or services! You can explore:

- The need that the prospective client has;
- What they will notice is different once the need has been met;
- Other challenges they face at the moment;
- People involved, and what they will notice;
- Existing resources that are part of this need;
- Any constraints or anticipated hurdles to overcome.

In this conversation, a full picture is developed, and may also generate referrals to others in your network who can help with the desired outcomes. If you are focusing on the need, and on the differences that will be noticed when the need has been met, you will open the conversation about Outcomes. If you can quantify the Outcomes in terms that are specific, observable and measurable, you are on your way to developing a specification for delivery.

At this stage, it may be that the outcomes are far from specific, appearing very broad and open. After all, there is an infinite number of outcomes and differences, so how do we find those that are likely to lead to a commercial transaction? For all the variety of outcomes, there are three areas of need where most transactions lie:

- The need to make more money;
- The need to save money;
- The need to save time.

Each of these delivers a Return on Investment – and if you are part of the delivery of outcomes that meet needs that make money, save money, save time or a combination of these, then it will be worth investing in your products or services.

Remember P, the Heating Engineer? Or David, the Vet Marketing Help Guy? Both of these providers offer a Return on Investment for their clients and that is what their clients are buying.

The Three Stage Buying Process

There is a three stage process that we all go through when we make a purchase, no matter what it is we buy.

As a buyer, our first question when we contemplate a purchase is, 'Does this product/service meet my needs?'

The second question we ask is, 'Does the brand or provider have credibility that they can meet my needs?'

At the point in the process where the buyer is answering 'YES!' to these questions, the third question asked is, 'Can I afford it?'.

This last question is often a surprise to people. We live in a world where people are obsessed by the price of things. This leads many people to starting a business where their point of difference to their competitors is simply to be cheaper. For a start, trying to simply compete on price will always be won by the competitor with the deepest pockets. Second, it is unlikely that anyone will want to refer the cheapest service. Ask yourself honestly, would you like a referral to the cheapest dentist in town?

Major brands have known about this for ages and forgive me for not referring to my source of this wisdom. If anyone can advise me who developed this model, please let me know and I will gladly give them credit! Suffice to say I learned this from another source during my early career, and have applied it diligently in my own business, when supporting clients, and now in outlining my methods in this book.

For example, Apple Computers have long been more expensive than Windows PCs. If absolute price was the defining factor, no-one would purchase Apple Computers except those who really needed their graphical capacity and capability. Even then, the software they run is now available on both platforms so there is no advantage to their own proprietary operating system which was their point of difference for a long time.

So there must be a good reason for people buying Apple Computers, and in my opinion, it is in the brand. Apple Computers has invested heavily in developing their brand values and promoting them relentlessly. They seldom mention their products, and they certainly never talk about the technical specifications. Their focus is always on the differences their products make, and the ways in which their clients are different by using their products. As a result, their credibility is massive, and the credibility of someone who uses an Apple Computer is also high in the opinion of those who care about the equipment their clients or suppliers use.

This is an important principle to apply to ourselves and our own business, and to illustrate this, let's look at the investment we are making in marketing. In all aspects, we need to ask ourselves if our marketing is enhancing the credibility of our personal brand. While we might not have millions to spend on TV campaigns, we do have control over how we present ourselves to the world. In our immediate network, our credibility is reflected in the way we present ourselves. This includes the way we dress, style our hair, the language we use, and whether or not we are good company in conversation. There is no set formula for this, and in a book designed to help you escape labels, there is no need to conform to one single stereotype. However, if you are looking to help a specific group of people as identified in your URP, you need to present your brand in such a way that you have credibility with your prospective clients, and with your network so that they can introduce you with confidence.

A clear way to do this is to be mindful of your on-line presence. There are too many social media platforms to list here, however if you have identified those that are likely to be enjoyed by your URP clients, you need to ensure that your own presence on these platforms enhances your credibility. Be aware that people will check you out, and in particular they will check you out if you are referred to them. If their first impressions chime with the referral, your credibility will be enhanced before you are even calling them.

Most new businesses invest in a website, business cards, and some other promotional materials. After all, we have all been told that we need to spend money wisely on 'marketing'. I recommend that you look at your marketing items and ensure that the contents enhance your credibility. If you have any items that include a long list of 'What We Do', I hope that by now you will have revised that into some specific examples of 'How We Help'. Consider your website solely as a credibility enhancer, and you will find it much easier to populate with relevant content. This approach will also save you money on items you don't need, and will help you spend money on those you do. For example, many people starting a business will invest money in leaflets, and then get the cheapest business cards they can. If you are contemplating (or already distributing) leaflets, can I just ask what you do with the leaflets that come through your door? Exactly. Given the choice, a quality business card will help when you are introduced to the specific clients that fit your URP, and if you need additional materials, ensure they are credibility enhancing and that they are appropriate for your URP clients.

Looking at our own businesses, you may have wondered why I spent some time adding preliminary steps to the process of calling a prospective client to whom you have been referred. Well, the answer is that the first phone call, and the subsequent first meeting are essential parts of starting the three-stage buying process.

Unless you are already spending millions on credibility building marketing, it is likely that you are solely responsible for your personal credibility. If you start your relationship with your new prospective client in a credibility enhancing way, you are starting to build your chances of being engaged from day one.

When you get to your first meeting and you are exploring the need, the noticeable differences, the outcomes, the other people, resources and constraints or barriers, you are building your credibility by showing interest in the client.

By the way, did you notice that there was something missing here?

At no stage should you start a conversation with a prospective client by talking about yourself, your business, your products and services. On no circumstances should you prepare a presentation, or a pitch, or any other form of sales device in advance of a first meeting. Does that surprise you? If you follow this system so far, I won't need to explain that this form of 'selling' involves you guessing what the client needs, and then hoping that they will work out how one of the many things you present actually meets their needs.

As an example, I delivered this method in a training course in 2016 to a group of around 150 BNI® members in Yorkshire. This was the first time I had delivered this course, and on the basis of feedback I received, it went well. A few weeks later, at another BNI® Course, a member called F came up to me and shook my hand, thanking me for the course I had delivered a few weeks previously. F told me his story.

He had a client meeting the morning after my training course, and in the traditional way, he had prepared his presentation and his pitch. He was aware he was competing against two rival commercial finance experts, and he was majoring on how price competitive he could be. He was planning to win the business by being cheaper.

After my course, he had second thoughts. He went to the client meeting the next morning, and he did not produce his presentation, nor deliver his pitch. Instead, he showed interest in the client, asked lots of questions about his needs, desired outcomes, and his challenges and priorities. He did not offer a price but took away a clear view of the client's requirements and offered to return with a specification of how he thought he could help. At the later training course, F came up to shake my hand because the approach worked. The client hired F, and when asked for his reasons, he simply told him that he was the only one of the three companies who had shown interest in him, and he felt that F's approach was more tailored to his needs.

You see, the client was not interested in price. He was actually interested in time. And he was happy to pay more to a provider who could save him time, and F was able to offer that service. F is still working on that project with the client now, and it is expected that this will be five years' work, earning a substantial six-figure sum.

What about the Price?

In the first phone call, or in the first meeting, chances are your client will ask you for your prices. Whatever you do, don't give them what they are asking for. Answering this question too early in the buying process will kill the conversation stone dead.

Going through the buying process is (once again), related to the process of dating. As I mentioned earlier, if you lay everything on the table in the first meeting, you have no opportunity to explore anything other than the price. Your client has no means of comparing you to others than price. And neither you nor they know whether your price is correct, as you don't actually know whether you can help them, nor what you can do for them. So how can you talk about price?

On the subject of which, here are two consultants. A charges £300 per day and B charges £800 per day. Which one are you going to hire?

Now, having established your needs and your outcomes, A will require 10 days to complete the work to your satisfaction, while B will complete this in two.

Which consultant are you going to hire now?

By the way, if you are just thinking B because they are £1400 cheaper, you are half right. B will also deliver the outcomes eight days' earlier than A, adding the value of the outcome to your business so you get an increased return more quickly.

Developing Credibility

Unless you are spending millions on your brand marketing, a method is needed to develop your credibility. Already, there are many credibility enhancing elements that have gone into the referral. These include:

- ✓ It's a word of mouth referral
- ✓ The story supporting the referral
- ✓ The background checks the client has done on your marketing and media
- ✓ The initial phone call you made

So now that you are in conversation with your client, you are establishing an interest in their needs and outcomes, and this conversation will also enhance your credibility. You get to the point where you have clearly identified their needs, and they are receptive to your approach. So far, so good.

And then they ask you for the price.

At this point, the temptation is to give them a price. So what do you say? Do you tell them your daily rate? Your standard off the peg price? How do you know this will do the job?

At this point, I always step away from giving a price. Instead, I offer to create a specification. This is a simple document consisting of the following:

1. The Outcomes Identified

2. The Noticeable Differences Sought
3. The Delivery Method Discussed
4. Any other matters *relevant to the project specification*
5. The follow up paragraph

This document is to all intent the basis of your proposal, however the important element that is missing is the price. There is a very good reason for this.

The follow up paragraph should be something like:

'I trust that this is an accurate specification of your requirements, and of the products/services we will provide to meet your needs. I will call you to make sure that this is the case, and to answer any questions.'

I am indebted to Andy Bounds, author of 'The Jelly Effect' and 'The Snowball Effect' for his question to the BNI® conference audience of which I was a member, 'Which would you prefer, a short proposal or a long proposal?'. There is no advantage in filling your document with details about your company, your services, your car parking arrangements, your team, your customer service offer, or the brand of coffee you are proud to serve to your visitors. None of this is anything to do with the client's desired outcomes, so omit it completely.

I am also grateful to Andy for the process of leaving the discussion of the price until you are sure that the specification meets the client's needs which I have adopted and adapted here. The step of submitting a price free specification is essential to the process of building credibility, and it also leaves open the opportunity to follow up. As with the first meeting question, as soon as price enters the discussion, the conversation stops. You are asking your client to accept your price and say 'Yes' or reject your price and say 'No'. There is no opportunity to revise the specification and to amend the price.

If there is no price on the table, then when you follow up, your call will be taken. Your client knows that you are checking to see that the specification meets their needs, and that you have demonstrated a clear understanding of their desired outcomes. At every stage you are enhancing your credibility, increasing the chances of your client answering 'Yes' to the first two questions of the three-stage buying process.

Moving to the Price

Having revised the specification together, you will eventually get to the point where you have no further changes to make. At this point, you can ask the client, 'So is this exactly what you are looking for?' or words to that effect. If the client says, 'Yes', you can now offer your price. If the specification is not clear, then of course you can review, if needs be reviewing the outcomes too.

The proposal you send is the revised specification with the addition of your price, and the administration such as invoicing and payment preferences. You have already established that the specification is what the client wants in order to meet their needs, and so you should be able to give an accurate price for this product or service.

The Decision

If you have established outcomes that save time, save money or make money, then have co-created the specification to deliver these, your price should be met with one of two responses.

First would be an acceptance, and discussion can move on to implementation.

Second would be, 'Sorry, we can't afford it.'

If you get either of these responses, the good news is that you have followed the process, and both are successful outcomes for you. By following the process, you have somewhere to go to if you are told your client can't afford it.

At this stage, you are unlikely to be told that there is somebody cheaper providing an alternative. If there is, then it will be very hard for you to compete with them on price without getting into a price war, and it is highly likely that their price will be to a different specification. If your client is not on the same page as you are after all this time of co-creating your specification, you may simply be best to walk away and let them go elsewhere. If it doesn't work out with the competitor, they might be back to you soon. In any case, you get to move onto the next thing.

More likely is that the client will be keen to work with you, and is simply stating the plain fact that they can't afford it. The process you have followed enables you to move this forward.

For a start, you have established that the outcomes are exactly what they want, and the specification you have proposed will deliver these. So, you can ask your client if they would like to revisit the outcomes. Reducing these will reduce your specification, reducing the fees you need for your products or services.

Second, you have the opportunity to phase the project. By now, your client may be happy to share the budget they can invest, after all you have told them clearly how much you charge for a given piece of work so you are entering into a professional relationship built on trust. Phasing the outcomes is a great way of moving forwards.

Either way, the conversation is maintained, even now that price is on the table.

One last thing. If a client is insistent that they want your price at the start of this conversational process, and you know now not to give it to them, you can always ask them to share the budget they had in mind. It may be that they do, in which case a collaborative relationship can be tried. Or it may be more likely that they are affronted at the suggestion. Well, if they are, you can simply say that until you have a specification, it is impossible for them to share their budget, nor for you to share your price, and then seek to move on to the outcomes and specification development conversations that we know will be useful.

By following the Unique Referral Point process, using the three stage buying process and remembering to delay discussing price until after the specification is agreed, your conversion rate will increase dramatically.

Implementation

There is a further advantage when the project is implemented, or the product created. Having identified the noticeable differences that will emerge when the outcomes are delivered, it is possible to notice these happening early in the project. This provides reassurance to all parties that the project is working. If the differences sought are not noticed early, changes can be made to the specification before it is too late. This massively enhances your credibility and saves you from pursuing a path that will not deliver the client's needs to the point where you are providing more products or services than were originally specified and costed.

ACTION POINTS

Next time you receive a referral, follow this process:

1. Contact the referrer for the story

2. Conduct background research

3. Phone prospect client and schedule a meeting

4. In the meeting explore the help they need and the outcomes they seek

5. If appropriate, co-create, submit, and then jointly develop a specification

6. Once Specification agreed, work out your price and submit a proposal

7. Shape the proposal to meet your client's budget

8. Review progress by measuring the noticeable differences identified

Helping with Transition

Successful athletes are amongst the most specific, dedicated and hard working people on the planet. Having found their sport, they spend every waking hour on fitness, skill development and nutrition programmes that are solely focused on being the best in their sport. And then they retire in their mid-thirties, or in some cases, even earlier, often not through their own choice if due to injury or to cuts in their funding. Having been an Olympian or Paralympian, a Footballer, Rugby Player or Cricketer, suddenly you are 'not' the label you have lived by all your adult life – yet you are known as having been one of these, and the label will stick. For every Gary Lineker who carves a new career in Media, there are hundreds more who retire each year and need to seek a new career as they enter the period of their lives that for most people is their most productive time.

For those who are not athletes, there are many transitions that will impact during our lives. Changes of job are often forced due to redundancy or retirement. It is seldom that I hear someone celebrating when they have lost their job, and the Label that went with it.

A major part of the label is status. It is for this reason that there are so many important sounding labels, particularly in corporate world. Where once there was an Account Manager, now there is a Business Development Manager. I even have a friend who has the title 'Head of Customer Excellence', whatever that may mean! And of course the status that comes from being an Olympic or Paralympic athlete, a Professional Footballer, Rugby Player or Cricketer is massive. As well as the financial rewards (real or perceived), there is a profile in the media and on social media, and the support (and criticism) that comes from having people who are your fans and supporters.

It is a similar situation for those who have a career. At events people will ask each other what they do. Our parents like to be able to tell their friends what we are doing. Our passport asks you for your profession and expects you to complete it with a label. As a society, we are keen on labels. So how do we manage the transition when our label changes, perhaps through no desire on our part for it to change? Or what if you have pro-actively decided you need to make a change?

I know from my own experience, and conversations with many that there is a mid-point in our careers where we contemplate our options. In our early stages where everything is possible, we have boundless energy, no commitments, and we can climb the career ladder with confidence. However in the middle stages, while some continue to progress, for many a plateau is reached. This may be a very comfortable plateau involving a good remuneration package and perceived security, however there is something missing. We are unlikely to be enjoying a seven-day weekend, so we invest time and money in maximising our leisure time, and holidays in particular. We look at our colleagues in the later stages of their careers and all they talk about is their plans for retirement. Their eyes light up when they mention the plan to travel, visit friends and family, take up a neglected hobby, learn a new skill or academic discipline, and of course spend time 'enjoying themselves'.

If you are in this position, consider the application of the URP to your employed position. You may be able to find positions within your existing employer that give you more of the differences you seek. You may be able to find a role with another employer that will do this too. Perhaps you are in a position to step out of employment and start developing your own income through working for yourself. However you choose to make a transition, being true to yourself will help you in all aspects of your life.

When considering professional sports people, or other age restricted activities, all of the changes I outline above are forced upon them and there is usually time to plan for this transition. I hope that if you have read the rest of this book up until now, you will be considering your options to make a proactive change. At the very least, I hope this will leave you better prepared should change be made for you.

The first step I recommend is to take stock of yourself as a whole person, and to think beyond the label. Following the process in this book, ask yourself what you are passionate about? What do you love doing? How do you help others? What are your core values?

For an athlete at the top of their profession, chances are that they will answer with 'doing the sport'! However what is it about 'doing the sport' that you love? When you are doing the sport, what do you notice about yourself? If you ask yourself this question, and then ask What else? until you have over 50 noticeable and measurable differences you observe about yourself, you will have a clear picture of the benefits you realise when you do your sport. You can apply this process whatever your discipline. And if you find that carrying on with your current chosen path delivers most of these noticeable differences, that is fantastic news. You can consider yourself refreshed as you make the most of the next stage in your career.

Now let's look at the interactional element. What are the differences others notice when you do your thing? Identify the people you interact with. We all have friends and family, colleagues and professional contacts. We also all have members of the public involved to a greater or lesser degree either as supporters, or as customers. So what would they notice about you when you do your thing? If you ask this question and start listing, you should need a lot of paper! Remember, we are looking for observable and measurable differences – list them now.

The first list you have created is how you help yourself and the second is how you help others when you do the thing you do.

My best hope for this line of questioning is that you have now thought of occasions when you were not doing the thing you are passionate about or have been labelled for, yet you are noticing the differences which are integral to your passion, or the label by which you have lived. It is in this process that we can identify new directions that will deliver these differences, helping to transition from one Label to the next.

Dame Kelly Holmes is an amazing example of making the transition successfully – though she found it a massive struggle and has documented the mental health challenges she faced. From a decorated career in the Army and scaling the heights of athletics to be Double Olympic Champion in Athens 2004, Dame Kelly now runs a community café where she is giving back to the community that nurtured her, as well as an institution that helps athletes to make the transition when their athletics career ends.

Hearing her on a programme on Radio 4 recently (One-to-One, 9th July 2018), she spoke of always wanting to make a difference in her community. The building she now runs as a community café was a bookshop when she was a child, and she knew from an early age that she wanted to buy this building – even though she didn't know why. Fourteen years after her double Olympic success she is now running this café.

Dame Kelly had a passion for giving to the community that she has fulfilled while in the Army, while a top Athlete, and now as proprietor of a Community Café in addition to her charitable activities. She managed to find the difference she wanted to make to help others, and has successfully made that difference despite her label changing as her career changed with experience and age. So can we apply this learning to our own situation in the context of the methods I have outlined?

For me, this story started in August 2006. Like many I know, I had followed a career path that conformed to what was considered sensible, and most importantly that met the approval of my parents! I went to University mainly because it was expected. I selected to study Electronics and Electrical Engineering as it was expected that my degree would help me find employment at the end. I was lucky enough to join Unilever post-graduation, and after a comprehensive training scheme, I enjoyed management roles in Engineering and then in Sales. I left Unilever to join Bass Brewers Ltd, and after two years as a Sales Manager, I helped to launch and then manage a dot.com, barbox.com, which became the on-line ordering platform for the UK Licensed On-Trade. At the age of 38 years, I had a good job, good pension, health insurance, company car, holiday entitlement, and a healthy salary with a good chance of a bonus each year. And then I walked into the office one day and saw my future.

There in the office sat my colleagues who were around 50 years' old. Whenever we went out socially (which in the hospitality business was often), they would share with me their plans for their retirement, and their faces would light up as they described often very detailed plans. However, I could see that nearly all of them were bored. They had reached the point where they were counting the days to retirement, and as I walked into the office that morning, a light bulb flashed in my mind. This was my future in front of me.

I was 38 years' old. I could retire comfortably at 60, with a final salary pension that would have funded a very happy retirement. However, for over five years, I had commuted from my home to the office, a 200 mile (300km) round trip that required me to stay away from home two or three nights per week. I was driving 45,000 miles (70,000km) per annum, so perhaps unsurprisingly, my back injury was not getting any better. And my future career path would involve either moving house to be nearer the office, or continuing with the punishing schedule so that after another 22 years, I could then start enjoying myself.

With no particular plan in mind, I left my employment, and for the first time in my life, I took some time out for me.

I spent some time building a kitchen. I helped my friend Jim Reilly to set up a new web development company, Easy Web Sites Ltd, which is still going strong today. Jim joined BNI® in Preston, and sponsored me to join in Leeds, which I did in December 2009. We were self-funding the new business, so I needed to find work. I was appointed a BizFizz Coach in Bradford in March 2007, and following the formal coaching skills training, I discovered I had been coaching all my life (as a survival skill) and this was my natural home. One of my first clients was the late Greg Vinnicombe. Greg introduced me to Solution Focused Practice, and we worked together as associates until his untimely death in October 2015. When the funding for the Bradford project finished, I set up my own company so that I could carry on as a coach and could bring the BizFizz Enterprise Coaching model to other communities as a freelance consultant. I am grateful to my colleagues in BNI® as without their support, and the experience of the BNI® model, I doubt I would have had the bravery to set up on my own.

For the first five years of my membership, I was one of those who, since Coaches can help anyone with anything, refused the BNI® training and advice to be specific in my regular referral requests. Then, I was hired by Jo Shepheard, the Charity Manager of CandleLighters', a charity that supports the families of children with cancer who live in Yorkshire. This turned into two years' of support work, and while CandleLighters' developed and grew, so I realised that once again, I had found the place I wanted to make a difference. I started asking for referrals to Charities and Community Companies, and for five years now, have developed my URP in this area. Across my network, I am known as 'the guy who helps Charities', and as a result receive the referrals I want every week.

I also receive referrals to people looking to start businesses, or make a living from self-employment, my other URPs.

When I receive referrals that don't fit my URP, I happily pass on to those better qualified and so I generate referrals for my network of coaches as well as other service providers and trades.

Over time, it is possible to discover new URPs, and to develop them too. For example, I have recently started working with a Franchise Owner to help them help their Franchisees, and so this could be a new URP for me to develop in 2019.

If you are in that position of seeking a change, seeking inspiration, or simply being bored where you are now and contemplating your options, I hope this book will help you to see that there are many different ways you can make a living. I am lucky enough to look forward to Monday mornings (and Tuesdays, and Wednesdays), and as I write this on a Saturday morning, I really can't say I would prefer to be doing something else.

Conclusion

We live in a society where labels are appended by others, and usually for their own reasons. Politicians apply their own labels to people they think will vote for them; government agencies apply labels to large groups of people and then try to meet their individual needs with a single solution; communities are labelled and as a result, discriminated against by those who think they can; and in the world of work, our label defines our place in society, in the hierarchy, and is a means of finding meaning in what we do.

Well, my approach involves ripping up the labels.

As human beings, we are so much more than the sum of all our labels. Our social capital develops from our networks, our interaction with our networks, and our ability to help others. Through our awareness of the differences we can make for and with others, we can achieve satisfaction with our selves, leading to emotional fulfilment and the many benefits that can bring to our health, and the well-being of those closest to us.

If you are at school and being asked 'what you want to do?' it is OK if you don't know, and it will be OK if at some point you change your mind.

If you are at University and you wish to change your course, or leave, that is OK. If you define yourself by how you help others, you will find a way to help others without the need for the degree.

If you are on the career ladder and dreading Monday mornings, it is OK to contemplate other directions. While you may have status and remuneration that goes with your label, it is OK to reconsider the differences you make in society, and to find those that are closest to your heart.

If you are paused in your career at the level you know is your last, and yet you still have many years until retirement, it is OK to find ways of making a difference that will provide you with fulfilment sooner rather than later.

If you are in need of help from another, it is OK to ask for help with finding the differences you seek. I hope you find someone who has read this book too, so that they are helping you for the differences it will make for you both.

Andrew Gibson